KATHRYN HAWKINS AND JENNY STACEY

RISOTTO

OVER 120 HEALTHY AND DELICIOUS "LITTLE RICE" RECIPES

FIREFLY BOOKS

A FIREFLY BOOK

Published by Firefly Books Ltd., 2000

First Printing

Canadian Cataloguing in Publication Data
Stacey, Jenny
Risotto : over 120 healthy and delicious "little rice" recipes
Includes index.
ISBN 1-55209-538-X
1. Cookery (Rice). 2. Risotto. I. Hawkins, Kathryn, 1996- .
II. Title.
TX809.R5S72 2000   641.6'318   C99-932741-0

U.S. Cataloging in Publication Data
Stacey, Jenny
Risotto : over 120 healthy and delicious "little rice" recipes /
Jenny Stacey and Kathryn Hawkins. —1st ed.
[114] p. : col. ill. ; cm.–
Includes index.
ISBN 1-55209-538-X
1. Cookery (Rice). I. Hawkins, Kathryn. II. Title.
641.6/318 –dc21   2000   CIP

First published in Canada in 2000
by Firefly Books Ltd.
3680 Victoria Park Avenue
Willowdale, Ontario
M2H 3KI

Published in the United States in 2000
by Firefly Books (U.S.) Inc.
P.O. Box 1338, Ellicott Station
Buffalo, New York 14205

This book was designed and produced by
Quintet Publishing Limited
6 Blundell Street
London N7 9BH

Creative Director: Richard Dewing
Art Director: Simon Daley
Project Editor: Laura Price
Designer: Rod Teasdale
Editor: Pamela Ellis
Photographer: Paola Zucchi
Food Stylists: Julz Beresford and Kathryn Hawkins

Typeset in Great Britain by Central Southern Typesetters, Eastbourne
Manufactured in Hong Kong by Regent Publishing Services Ltd.
Printed in China by Leefung-Asco Printers Ltd.

CONTENTS

ALL ABOUT RISOTTO

RISOTTO" MEANS "**LITTLE RICE**." IT IS AN ITALIAN DISH THAT CAN BE FLAVORED WITH MEAT, POULTRY, FISH, VEGETABLES, SHELLFISH, AND GAME AND SERVED AS A MAIN COURSE OR APPETIZER.

Risotto is cooked in a large wide pan in stock, or a mixture of stock and wine, and flavored with the ingredients described. It may also be simply flavored with cheese or saffron and served as a side dish. The most famous example is risotto alla Milanese, which is traditionally served with *Osso Buco*. Whether risotto is served as the appetizer, main course, or even dessert, the remainder of the meal should be light.

Rice, the basis of risotto, is nutritious as well as delicious. Being a complex carbohydrate, it contains starch and fiber and is digested slowly. It is also a good source of potassium and the B vitamins niacin and thiamin. A 2-ounce (50-gram) raw portion of rice also provides

approximately 10% of an adult's R.D.A. of protein. Containing virtually no cholesterol or fat, rice is ideal for those watching their fat intake. It is also gluten-free, making it suitable for people who suffer from celiac disease. Additional ingredients may increase fat and calorie counts, however, so it should not always be considered healthy, especially if cream or high-fat meat is added.

Risottos are one of the most delicious yet simplest of Italian dishes. The technique of cooking short-grain rice is traditional and involves stirring hot stock gradually into the rice. A variety of ingredients are added to the basic risotto recipe to produce many combinations of color, flavor, and texture. Because rice is so filling, a risotto makes an economical meal for a family, its versatility never allowing for boredom. Risottos are best eaten freshly cooked, but some may be frozen if their flavorings allow. In this case, do not completely cook the rice, cool it, then freeze. Defrost risotto thoroughly and reheat with additional butter or oil until completely hot right through, and creamy in texture.

In the Veneto region of Italy, the dish is so popular it commands its own festival. The four-day celebration enables guests to taste a host of risotto recipes, and competition for the best recipe is fierce. Risotto is cooked on the streets in huge iron pans, and guests are invited to indulge at their will.

some essentials

To achieve the characteristic creamy consistency of risotto, there are a few points to consider. The first and most important of these is the type of rice used.

THE RICE The high starch quantity of these grains allows them to absorb liquid slowly, resulting in a creamy texture without a loss of bite. It is therefore important that the rice is not washed before cooking or some of the starch will be removed and the texture of the finished dish will be more grainy. Long-grain rice will not give the desired result. To achieve the required texture, only authentic risotto rice should be used for these recipes. This is not a problem as the most common one, arborio rice, is widely available. There are three risotto rices that are all grown in Italy. The first of these is *Vialone nano*, a medium-grain, round rice which is grown in the Veneto. It has a less creamy texture than the following varieties. *Arborio* rice is a plump,

longer-grained rice from Piedmont. It will absorb a high quantity of liquid without losing its *al dente* bite, and is classed as a "superfino" rice. It gives a delicious, creamy result. The final rice, *carnaroli*, is a smaller superfino-grain rice than arborio and is from the Lombardy region. It too will absorb large quantities of liquid without becoming soggy.

THE STOCK The second point to consider when making risotto is the stock. If possible, use a good homemade stock, varying the flavor according to the recipe. Use fish, beef, chicken, lamb, vegetable, or pork stock. If this is not possible, aim to use a good-quality prepared stock. This will add fantastic flavor to the dish as the rice absorbs it while cooking.

THE PAN Thirdly, choose your pan carefully. A wide heavy-based pan is best. It should be quite deep to help to slow the evaporation of the liquid, but not so deep that it is difficult to stir the risotto thoroughly.

cooking risotto

The correct heat should be maintained during cooking. If the dish is cooked on too high a heat, the liquid will evaporate too quickly for the rice to absorb it. If too low a heat is used, slow cooking will give a soggy result and the rice will not cook evenly. A perfect risotto is neither too runny nor too dry, but tender and creamy, with the grains holding together, yet separate.

The actual cooking method is simple, but requires constant attention. Here are a few tips to consider for the perfect risotto.

First, heat the stock, or stock and wine, if using a mixture, to boiling point. Reduce the heat to maintain a gentle simmer throughout the cooking time. Adding hot liquid makes the rice grains swell, but keeps them firm. It also ensures the continuous cooking of the rice. If cold liquid is added, the rice will take longer to cook and the required texture will not be obtained.

When you begin to prepare your risotto and fry your onion it is important not to let the onion brown because the dish will be too sweet and the color will be wrong.

When the rice is coated in the butter and oil mixture, add a small quantity of hot stock to the rice and stir it in until it is completely absorbed. After this, continue to add the hot stock in small quantities, allowing for absorption in between. Constant stirring ensures that the rice evenly absorbs the liquid and maintains an even consistency while cooking.

Do not try to rush the cooking process by turning up the heat or adding the stock more quickly. This will simply ruin the final dish.

The liquid quantities and timings of the recipes given in this book are approximate. Some dishes may require more or less liquid and a longer or shorter cooking time, depending on the heat, the pan used, the type of rice, and the other ingredients.

serving risotto

Ideally, the risotto should rest for a few minutes before serving in warm, shallow bowls or plates. It is often served with freshly grated Parmesan, topped with fresh herbs and accompanied by a glass of Italian wine.

The recipes here demonstrate the versatility of this delicious dish, covering a range of dishes using vegetables, meat, poultry, fish and shellfish, and game. Each recipe serves 4 as a main course or 6 to 8 as an appetizer or side dish.

There are even some sweet fruit and chocolate recipes, that will make a perfect finale to a meal, each serving 4 as dessert.

making the perfect basic risotto

1 Heat the stock, then cook onion, garlic, and other flavorings in butter or butter and oil, in a large shallow pan. Stir in the unwashed rice and cook, stirring constantly, for 2 minutes. Keep the rice moving in the pan until it is well-coated in the butter and oil. This will ensure the rice cooks evenly and is well-flavored.

2 The stock or other liquid(s) should be added in small quantities. Allowing the rice to absorb the liquid between each addition is vital for the creamy texture that is characteristic of risotto. Once the stock has been added, if the risotto becomes too dry, add hot water. It should take approximately 20 minutes for the dish to cook after this initial addition of stock.

3 The risotto is ready to eat when a creamy texture has been achieved . The rice should be firm to the bite, but tender. It should be neither chalky nor soggy. Add butter or any further ingredients, garnish, and serve.

4 Some risottos benefit from *mantecare* – being covered and left to rest for several minutes when ready, with extra butter or cheese, or both, stirred in. This makes the texture even more creamy.

VEGETARIAN RISOTTO

Mediterranean Vegetable Risotto
Risotto Verde
Risotto Rosso
Risotto Giallo
Risotto Bianco
Asparagus Risotto
Green Vegetable Risotto
Olive and Caper Tomato Risotto
Olive Risotto
Risotto with Squash
Blue Cheese Pumpkin Risotto
Risotto alla Milanese
Cheese and Sun-dried Tomato Risotto
Orange Fennel Risotto
Lemon Shallot Risotto
Orange, Sage and Mushroom Risotto
Buttery Pumpkin and Hazelnut Risotto
Walnut, Garlic and Thyme Risotto
Fragrant Herb Risotto
Mixed Onion Risotto
Spinach and Raisin Risotto
Four-cheese Risotto
Spinach and Gorgonzola Risotto
Saffron, Bell Pepper and Marsala Risotto
Red Onion Tomato Risotto
Mixed Vegetable and Bean Risotto
Pilaf-style Risotto
Risotto con Vermicelli
Chili Bean Risotto
Oriental Vegetable Risotto

mediterranean vegetable risotto

THIS RISOTTO MAKES A STUNNING MAIN COURSE. FOR A SIMPLE MEAL, SERVE WITH HERB OR CHEESE BREAD.

1 medium eggplant

2 medium zucchini

1 red bell pepper

2 medium tomatoes

1 red onion

2 cloves garlic

6 Tbsp (75 mL) olive oil

2 Tbsp (25 mL) chopped fresh or
  2 tsp (10 mL) dried rosemary

5 cups (1.25 L) vegetable stock

1 medium onion, finely chopped

2 cups (500 mL) arborio rice

²/₃ cup (150 mL) dry white wine

Salt and freshly ground black pepper

¹/₃ cup (90 mL) diced or crumbled
  feta cheese

Fresh rosemary, to garnish

1 First prepare the vegetables. Trim and dice the eggplant into 1-in (2.5-cm) pieces. Trim and slice the zucchini. Seed and dice the bell pepper into 1-in (2.5-cm) cubes. Quarter the tomatoes. Peel and cut the red onion into 8 wedges. Peel and thinly slice the garlic.

2 Place all the vegetables in a bowl and gently stir in 5 Tbsp (65 mL) olive oil and the rosemary until well-mixed. Preheat the broiler. Broil the vegetables for 8 to 10 minutes, turning frequently, until lightly charred and tender. Set aside.

3 Pour the stock into a saucepan and bring to a boil. Reduce the heat to a gentle simmer.

4 Meanwhile, heat the remaining oil in a large saucepan and gently fry the onion for 2 to 3 minutes until softened. Add the rice and cook, stirring, for 2 minutes until well-coated in the onion mixture.

5 Add the wine and cook gently, stirring, until absorbed. Ladle in the stock gradually, until all the liquid is absorbed and the rice is thick, creamy, and tender. Keep the heat moderate. This will take about 25 minutes. Season well.

6 Gently stir in the prepared vegetables and heat through for 2 to 3 minutes until hot. Serve sprinkled with the cheese and garnished with fresh rosemary.

risotto verde

THIS FRESH-TASTING DISH IS THE PERFECT
ACCOMPANIMENT TO FISH AND POULTRY DISHES.

- 5 cups (1.25 L) vegetable stock
- 2 Tbsp (25 mL) vegetable oil
- 1 large onion, finely chopped
- 2 green bell peppers, seeded and chopped
- 2 cups (500 mL) arborio rice
- $2/3$ cup (150 mL) dry white wine
- 2 cups (500 mL) frozen or freshly shelled peas
- 2 tsp (10 mL) ground coriander
- Salt and freshly ground black pepper
- 4 Tbsp (50 mL) chopped fresh cilantro
- 2 scallions, finely chopped

1 Pour the stock into a saucepan and bring to a boil. Reduce the heat to a gentle simmer.

2 Meanwhile, heat the oil in a large saucepan and gently fry the onion and bell peppers for 3 to 4 minutes until just softened but not browned. Add the rice and cook, stirring, for 2 minutes until well-coated in the pepper mixture.

3 Add the wine and cook gently, stirring, until absorbed. Ladle in the stock gradually, until half the liquid is absorbed. Mix in the peas. Continue ladling in the stock until the rice is thick, creamy, and tender. The heat should be moderate. This will take about 25 minutes.

4 Stir in the ground coriander and seasoning. Then mix in the fresh cilantro and serve sprinkled with the finely chopped scallions.

risotto rosso

THE VIBRANT COLOR OF THIS DISH COMES FROM THE
FRESH BEET. SERVE WITH SOUR CREAM, CRUSTY BREAD,
AND FRESHLY STEAMED GREEN VEGETABLES.

- 5 cups (1.25 L) vegetable stock
- 2 Tbsp (25 mL) butter
- 1 Tbsp (15 mL) olive oil
- 2 medium red onions, thinly sliced
- 4 medium fresh raw beets, peeled and shredded or coarsely grated
- 2 cups (500 mL) coarsely grated carrot
- 2 cups (500 mL) arborio rice
- $2/3$ cup (150 mL) red wine
- Salt and freshly ground black pepper
- 4 Tbsp (50 mL) sour cream
- Snipped fresh chives, to garnish

1 Pour the stock into a saucepan and bring to a boil. Reduce the heat to a gentle simmer.

2 Meanwhile, melt the butter with the oil in a large saucepan and gently fry the onions, beet, and carrot for 10 minutes until just beginning to soften. Add the rice and cook, stirring, for 2 minutes until well-coated in the vegetable mixture.

3 Add the red wine and cook gently, stirring, until absorbed. Ladle in the stock gradually over moderate heat until all the liquid is absorbed and the rice is thick, creamy, and tender. This will take about 25 minutes.

4 Add seasoning to taste. Serve immediately, topped with sour cream and sprinkled with chives.

OPPOSITE RISOTTO ROSSO

risotto giallo

THE SUNNY COLORS IN THIS DISH WILL BRIGHTEN
UP ANY MEAL. FOR MAXIMUM IMPACT, SERVE THE
RISOTTO WITH CONTRASTING COLORED SALADS.

5 cups (1.25 L) vegetable
stock

2 Tbsp (25 mL) butter

1 Tbsp (15 mL) vegetable
oil

1 large onion, finely
chopped

1 yellow bell pepper,
seeded and chopped

8 oz (225 g) pumpkin or
yellow squash flesh,
diced

2 cups (500 mL) arborio
rice

Large pinch saffron

Salt and white pepper

12-oz (350-g) can corn,
drained

Halved grilled yellow
tomatoes, to garnish

1 Pour the stock into a saucepan and bring to a boil.
Reduce the heat to a gentle simmer.

2 Meanwhile, melt the butter with the oil in a large
saucepan and gently fry the onion, pepper, and
pumpkin for 4 to 5 minutes until just softened. Add the
rice and cook, stirring, for 2 minutes until the rice is
well-coated in the vegetable mixture.

3 Add a ladleful of stock and cook gently, stirring until
absorbed. Continue ladling in the stock until half of
it is used. Sprinkle in the saffron and seasoning. Mix in
the corn.

4 Continue adding the stock until all the liquid is
absorbed and the rice is thick, creamy, and tender.
Keep the heat moderate. This will take about 25 minutes.
Garnish with the tomatoes and serve.

risotto bianco

THIS RISOTTO IS A SIMPLE COMBINATION OF MUSHROOMS
AND RICE WITH JUST A HINT OF THYME AND CREAM.

5 cups (1.25 L) vegetable
stock

1/4 cup (50 mL) garlic and
herb butter

1 medium onion, finely
chopped

1 clove garlic, minced

3 cups (750 mL) sliced
button or wild
mushrooms

1 tsp (5 mL) dried or 4 tsp
(20mL) fresh thyme

2 cups (500 mL) arborio
rice

Salt and white pepper

4 Tbsp (50 mL) extra-dry
vermouth

4 Tbsp (50 mL) heavy
cream

Fresh thyme, to garnish

1 Pour the stock into a saucepan and bring to a boil.
Reduce the heat to a gentle simmer.

2 Meanwhile, melt the butter and gently fry the onion,
garlic, mushrooms, and thyme for 3 to 4 minutes
until softened but not browned. Add the rice and cook,
stirring, for 2 minutes until well-coated in the mushroom
mixture. Season.

3 Add a ladleful of stock and cook gently, stirring,
until absorbed. Continue adding the stock, ladle by
ladle, until all the liquid is absorbed and the rice is thick,
creamy, and tender. Keep the heat moderate. This will
take about 25 minutes. Stir in the vermouth and cream.
Garnish and serve.

OPPOSITE RISOTTO BIANCO

asparagus risotto

LIGHTLY COOKED ASPARAGUS IS ADDED TO THIS
SIMPLE RISOTTO. IT CAN BE SERVED AS A
SUBSTANTIAL STARTER, SIDE DISH, OR SUPPER.

8 oz (225 g) asparagus
spears

5 cups (1.25 L) vegetable
stock (see method)

1 Tbsp (15 mL) olive oil

1 medium onion, finely
chopped

2 cups (500 mL) arborio
rice

4 Tbsp (50 mL) extra-dry
vermouth

4 Tbsp (50 mL) heavy
cream

Salt and freshly ground
black pepper

½ cup (125 mL) freshly
grated Parmesan cheese
(optional)

1 Cut off the very woody ends from the asparagus. Cut
the spears into 2-in (5-cm) lengths. Bring a small
saucepan of water to a boil and cook the asparagus for
4 to 5 minutes until just cooked. Drain and set aside.
Reserve the cooking liquid and use to make up the stock.

2 Pour the stock into a saucepan and bring to a boil.
Reduce the heat to a gentle simmer.

3 Meanwhile, heat the oil in a large saucepan and
gently fry the onion for 2 to 3 minutes until
softened but not browned. Add the rice and cook,
stirring, for 2 minutes.

4 Add a ladleful of stock and cook gently, stirring,
until absorbed. Continue ladling in the stock until
all the liquid has been absorbed and the rice is thick,
creamy, and tender. Keep the heat moderate. This will
take about 25 minutes.

5 Stir in the vermouth and cream. Gently mix in the
cooked asparagus and season. Serve sprinkled with
Parmesan, if using.

green vegetable risotto

MAKES AN EXCELLENT ACCOMPANIMENT TO MEAT OR FISH,
AND CAN ALSO BE SERVED AS A VEGETARIAN MAIN COURSE.

8 oz (225 g) small broccoli
florets

4 oz (125 g) fine asparagus
spears

8 oz (225 g) Savoy
cabbage, shredded

5 cups (1.25 L) vegetable
stock (see method)

¼ cup (50 mL) garlic and
herb butter

4 cups (1 L) trimmed and
shredded leeks

2 cups (500 mL) arborio
rice

Salt and freshly ground
black pepper

4 Tbsp (50 mL) chopped
fresh parsley

1 Bring a saucepan of water to a boil and cook the
broccoli for 3 to 4 minutes until just tender; cook
the asparagus and cabbage for 1 minute until just tender.
Reserving the cooking water, drain the vegetables and set
aside. Use the water to make up the stock.

2 Pour the stock into a saucepan and bring to a boil.
Reduce the heat to a gentle simmer.

3 Meanwhile, melt the garlic and herb butter in a large
saucepan and gently fry the leeks for 2 to 3 minutes
until softened but not browned. Stir in the rice and cook,
stirring, for 2 minutes until the rice is well-coated.

4 Add a ladleful of stock and cook gently over
moderate heat, stirring, until absorbed. Season well.
Continue adding the stock, ladle by ladle, until the risotto
is thick, but not sticky, and the rice is tender. This will
take about 25 minutes.

5 Stir in the cooked vegetables and chopped parsley,
and heat through for 2 to 3 minutes until hot.
Serve immediately.

OPPOSITE **ASPARAGUS RISOTTO**

olive & caper tomato risotto

THE TRADITIONAL COMBINATION OF INGREDIENTS IN THIS RISOTTO GIVES IT A THOROUGHLY ITALIAN FLAVOR.

3¾ cups (950 mL) vegetable stock

2 Tbsp (25 mL) olive oil

1 large onion, finely chopped

1 clove garlic, minced

2 cups (500 mL) arborio rice

1 tsp (5 mL) dried or 4 tsp (20mL) fresh mixed herbs

⅔ cup (150 mL) red wine

14-fl oz (398-g) can chopped tomatoes

Salt and freshly ground black pepper

1 cup (250 mL) pitted black olives

2 Tbsp (25 mL) capers

Romano cheese shavings, to garnish

1 Pour the stock into a saucepan and bring to a boil. Reduce the heat to a gentle simmer.

2 Meanwhile, heat the oil in a large saucepan and gently fry the onion and garlic for 2 to 3 minutes until softened but not browned. Add the rice and herbs and cook, stirring, for 2 minutes until well-coated in the onion mixture.

3 Add the wine and chopped tomatoes and cook gently, stirring, until absorbed. Ladle in the stock gradually and cook until all the liquid is absorbed and the rice is thick, creamy, and tender. This should take about 25 minutes.

4 Season well and stir in the olives and capers. Serve topped with shavings of Romano cheese and sprinkled with black pepper.

olive risotto

A MOUTH-WATERING COMBINATION OF RICE AND OLIVES MAKES THIS RISOTTO AN UNUSUAL SIDE DISH, OR, FOR AN OLIVE LOVER, THE PERFECT SUPPER.

5 cups (1.25 L) vegetable stock

3 Tbsp (45 mL) extra-virgin olive oil

8 oz (225 g) shallots, finely sliced

2 cloves garlic, minced

2 cups (500 mL) arborio rice

½ cup (125 mL) pitted green olives

½ cup (125 mL) pimento-stuffed green olives

¾ cup (200 mL) pitted black olives

Salt and freshly ground black pepper

2 Tbsp (25 mL) shredded basil leaves

1 Pour the stock into a saucepan and bring to a boil. Reduce the heat to a gentle simmer.

2 Meanwhile, heat 2 Tbsp (25 mL) oil in a large skillet and gently fry the shallots and garlic for 2 to 3 minutes until softened but not browned. Add the rice and cook, stirring, for 2 minutes until well-coated in the shallot mixture.

3 Add a ladleful of stock and cook gently, stirring, until absorbed. Continue adding the stock, ladle by ladle, into the rice until all the liquid has been absorbed and the rice is thick, creamy, and tender.

4 Stir in the olives and adjust the seasoning. Serve the risotto sprinkled with the basil and drizzled with the remaining oil.

OPPOSITE **OLIVE RISOTTO**

risotto with squash

SQUASH COMBINES WITH TOMATOES IN THIS
BUTTERY RISOTTO. SERVE THIS AS AN UNUSUAL
ACCOMPANIMENT TO A CASSEROLE, OR AS A
DELICIOUS ENTREE.

3¾ cups (950 mL)
vegetable stock

⅓ cup (90 mL) butter

2 medium red onions,
finely chopped

2 cloves garlic, minced

1 lb (450 g) butternut
squash flesh, diced

2 cups (500 mL) arborio
rice

Salt and freshly ground
black pepper

⅔ cup (150 mL) dry white
wine

14-fl oz (398-mL) can
chopped tomatoes

2 Tbsp (25 mL) chopped
fresh parsley

1 Pour the stock into a saucepan and bring to a boil.
Reduce the heat to a gentle simmer.

2 Meanwhile, melt the butter and gently fry the onion,
garlic, and squash for 7 to 8 minutes until just
softening. Add the rice and cook, stirring, for 2 minutes
until well-mixed. Season well.

3 Add the wine and chopped tomatoes and cook
gently, stirring, until absorbed. Add the stock, ladle
by ladle, until the liquid is absorbed and the rice is thick,
creamy, and tender. Keep the heat moderate. This will
take about 25 minutes.

4 Adjust the seasoning if necessary. Serve sprinkled
with chopped parsley.

blue cheese pumpkin risotto

PUMPKIN HAS AN EARTHY TASTE AND ABSORBS THE
FLAVORS FROM OTHER INGREDIENTS DURING COOKING. IN
THIS RISOTTO, IT COMBINES WITH BLUE CHEESE TO MAKE A
VERY RICH AND SURPRISINGLY DELICIOUS DISH.

5 cups (1.25 L) vegetable
stock

¼ cup (50 mL) butter

1 medium onion, finely
chopped

1 lb (450 g) pumpkin or
squash flesh, diced

2 cups (500 mL) arborio
rice

Salt and freshly ground
black pepper

½ cup (125 mL) crumbled
blue cheese, such as
Gorgonzola, Stilton, or
Danish blue

2 Tbsp (25 mL) chopped
fresh parsley

1 Pour the stock into a saucepan and bring to a boil.
Reduce the heat to a gentle simmer.

2 Meanwhile, melt the butter in a large saucepan and
gently fry the onion for 2 to 3 minutes until softened
but not browned. Add the pumpkin and continue to cook,
stirring, for 6 to 7 minutes until just beginning to soften.

3 Stir in the rice and cook, stirring, for 2 minutes until
the rice is well-coated in the pumpkin mixture. Add
the stock, ladle by ladle, until all the liquid is absorbed
and the rice is thick, creamy, and tender. Keep the heat
moderate. This will take about 25 minutes.

4 Season well and gently stir in the blue cheese. Serve
sprinkled with chopped parsley.

OPPOSITE BLUE CHEESE AND PUMPKIN RISOTTO

risotto alla milanese

RISOTTO ALLA MILANESE IS AN ITALIAN CLASSIC. GOLDEN YELLOW IN COLOR AND AROMATIC IN FLAVOR, THIS DISH CAN BE SERVED AS AN ACCOMPANIMENT OR AS A SUPPER WITH CRUSTY BREAD AND SALAD.

5 cups (1.25 L) vegetable stock

⅓ cup (90 mL) butter

1 medium onion, finely chopped

1 clove garlic, minced

2 cups (500 mL) arborio rice

Large pinch saffron

Salt and white pepper

1 cup (250 mL) freshly grated Parmesan cheese

1 Pour the stock into a saucepan and bring to a boil. Reduce the heat to a gentle simmer.

2 Meanwhile, melt ¼ cup (50 mL) butter in a large saucepan and gently fry the onion and garlic for 2 to 3 minutes until softened but not browned. Stir in the rice and cook, stirring, for 2 minutes, until well-coated in butter.

3 Add a ladleful of stock and cook gently, stirring, until absorbed. Continue adding the stock ladle by ladle to the rice until half the stock is used and the rice is creamy. Sprinkle in the saffron and seasoning.

4 Add the remaining stock until the risotto becomes thick, but not sticky. This will take about 25 minutes and should not be hurried. Just before serving, carefully stir in the remaining butter and the Parmesan cheese. Serve immediately.

OPPOSITE **RISOTTO ALLA MILANESE**

cheese & sun-dried tomato risotto

THIS IS AN EXTRA-RICH RISOTTO WITH THE DELICIOUS INTENSE TASTE OF SUN-DRIED TOMATOES, WHICH CAN BE SERVED AS A SIDE DISH OR AS A SIMPLE SUPPER.

½ cup (125 mL) soaked sun-dried tomatoes

5 cups (1.25 L) vegetable stock

¼ cup (50 mL) butter

1 medium onion, finely chopped

2 cups (500 mL) arborio rice

1 tsp (5 mL) dried or 4 tsp (20mL) fresh mixed herbs

Salt and freshly ground black pepper

¾ cup (200 mL) freshly grated Romano cheese

1-oz (25-g) piece Romano cheese

Flat leaf parsley, to garnish

1 Reserving the liquid, drain the tomatoes and slice into thin strips. Set aside.

2 Pour the stock into a saucepan and bring to a boil. Reduce the heat to a gentle simmer.

3 Meanwhile, melt the butter in a large saucepan and gently fry the onion and tomato for 2 to 3 minutes until softened but not browned. Stir in the rice and cook, stirring, for 2 minutes, until the rice is well-coated.

4 Add the tomato soaking liquid and cook gently, stirring until absorbed. Add the herbs and seasoning. Ladle in the stock, one ladleful at a time, until the liquid is absorbed and the rice is thick, creamy, and tender. This will take about 25 minutes.

5 Gently stir in the grated cheese and transfer to a warmed serving dish. Garnish with shaved cheese and parsley to serve.

orange fennel risotto

THIS IS A LIGHT AND FRAGRANT RISOTTO, PERFECT AS AN
APPETIZER OR DINNER DISH.

5 cups (1.25 L) vegetable
stock

2 bulbs fennel

2 Tbsp (25 mL) butter

1 Tbsp (15 mL) olive oil

2 sticks celery, trimmed
and chopped

2 medium leeks, trimmed
and shredded

2 cups (500 mL) arborio
rice

3 medium oranges

Salt and freshly ground
black pepper

1 Pour the stock into a saucepan and bring to a boil.
Reduce the heat to a gentle simmer.

2 Meanwhile, trim the fennel, reserving the fronds,
and cut into thin slices. Melt the butter with the oil
in a large saucepan and gently fry the fennel, celery, and
leeks for 3 to 4 minutes until just softened. Add the rice
and cook, stirring, for 2 minutes until well-mixed.

3 Add a ladleful of stock and cook gently, stirring,
until absorbed. Continue adding the stock, ladle by
ladle, until it is all absorbed and the rice becomes creamy,
thick, and tender. This will take about 25 minutes and
should not be hurried.

4 Remove the zest and extract the juice from 1 orange
and mix into the rice. Carefully slice off the peel and
pith from the remaining oranges and, holding the fruit
over the saucepan, slice out the orange sections and add
to the rice, along with any juice that falls. Gently mix into
the rice, season well, and serve garnished with the
reserved fennel fronds.

lemon shallot risotto

IN THIS DISH GOLDEN SHALLOTS ARE MIXED WITH THE
DELICATE FLAVORS OF LEMON AND FRESH TARRAGON.
THIS IS THE PERFECT RISOTTO WITH FISH OR SEAFOOD.

5 cups (1.25 L) vegetable
stock

1 Tbsp (15 mL) olive oil

2 Tbsp (25 mL) butter

8 oz (250 g) shallots,
halved

1 Tbsp (15 mL) lemon
juice

1 tsp (5 mL) sugar

2 cups (500 mL) arborio
rice

Finely grated zest of
1 lemon

Salt and freshly ground
black pepper

2 Tbsp (25 mL) chopped
fresh tarragon

4 Tbsp (50 mL) heavy
cream

1/2 cup (125 mL) freshly
grated Parmesan cheese

Fresh tarragon and lemon
zest, to garnish

1 Pour the stock into a saucepan and bring to a boil.
Reduce the heat to a gentle simmer.

2 Meanwhile, heat the oil and butter in a large
saucepan and fry the shallots with the lemon juice
and sugar for 6 to 7 minutes until golden brown and
lightly caramelized. Add the rice and cook, stirring, for
2 minutes until well-mixed.

3 Add a ladleful of stock and cook gently, stirring,
until absorbed. Continue adding the stock, ladle by
ladle, into the rice until half the stock is used and the
rice is creamy. Sprinkle in the lemon zest and seasoning.

4 Continue adding the stock until the risotto becomes
thick and the rice is tender. This will take about
25 minutes and should not be hurried. Stir in the
chopped tarragon, cream, and grated Parmesan cheese.
Adjust the seasoning if necessary. Garnish and serve.

OPPOSITE LEMON SHALLOT RISOTTO

orange, sage & mushroom risotto

TANGY ORANGE AND THE AROMATIC FLAVOR OF SAGE
ENLIVEN THIS MUSHROOM RISOTTO DISH.

3³/₄ cups (950 mL) vegetable stock

1/4 cup (50 mL) garlic and herb butter

2 Tbsp (25 mL) olive oil

1 medium onion, finely chopped

3 cups (750 mL) sliced mushrooms

2 large mushrooms, sliced

2 cups (500 mL) arborio rice

Salt and freshly ground black pepper

1 tsp (5 mL) powdered sage

1¹/₄ cups (300 mL) unsweetened orange juice

2 medium oranges

1 Tbsp (15 mL) chopped fresh sage

Orange zest, to garnish

1 Pour the stock into a saucepan and bring to a boil. Reduce the heat to a gentle simmer.

2 Meanwhile, melt the butter with the oil in a large saucepan and gently fry the onion and mushrooms for 3 to 4 minutes until just softened. Add the rice and cook, stirring, for 2 minutes until well-mixed. Season and add the powdered sage.

3 Add the orange juice and cook gently, stirring, until absorbed. Add the stock, ladle by ladle, until it is all absorbed and the rice is thick, creamy, and tender. Keep the heat moderate. This will take about 25 minutes.

4 Carefully peel the oranges, removing the pith at the same time. Holding the oranges over the risotto, slice out the orange sections and gently mix them into the rice. Adjust the seasoning, and mix in the chopped sage. Serve garnished with orange zest.

buttery pumpkin & hazelnut risotto

THIS DELICIOUS COMBINATION OF JUICY PUMPKIN,
NUTS, AND TANGY ORANGE MAKES A MEMORABLE
MAIN-COURSE DISH.

5 cups (1.25 L) vegetable stock

¹/₃ cup (90 mL) butter

1 large onion, finely chopped

1 lb (450 g) pumpkin flesh, diced

2 cloves garlic, minced

2 cups (500 mL) arborio rice

Grated zest of ¹/₂ orange

Salt and freshly ground black pepper

¹/₂ cup (125 mL) freshly grated Parmesan cheese

¹/₂ cup (125 mL) roasted chopped hazelnuts

Orange zest, to garnish

1 Pour the stock into a saucepan and bring to a boil. Reduce the heat to a gentle simmer.

2 Meanwhile, melt ¹/₄ cup (50 mL) butter in a large saucepan and gently fry the onion, pumpkin, and garlic for 7 to 8 minutes until just softened. Add the rice and cook, stirring, for 2 minutes until well mixed.

3 Add a ladleful of stock and cook gently, stirring, until absorbed. Continue adding the stock, ladle by ladle, until half is used and the rice is creamy. Add the grated orange zest and season.

4 Continue adding the stock until the risotto is thick and the rice is tender. This will take about 25 minutes. Stir in the remaining butter and grated cheese. Sprinkle with the hazelnuts and garnish with orange zest to serve.

OPPOSITE BUTTERY PUMPKIN RISOTTO

walnut, garlic & thyme risotto

THIS RISOTTO IS ENRICHED WITH WALNUTS AND THEIR OIL.
SERVE WITH A LIGHT GREEN SALAD.

5 cups (1.25 L) vegetable stock

2 Tbsp (25 mL) butter

1 Tbsp (15 mL) olive oil

4 cloves garlic, minced

1/2 cup (125 mL) very finely chopped walnuts

2 Tbsp (25 mL) chopped fresh thyme or 2 tsp (10 mL) dried

2 cups (500 mL) arborio rice

Salt and freshly ground black pepper

1 Tbsp (15 mL) walnut oil

1/2 cup (125 mL) walnut pieces

Sprig fresh thyme, to garnish

1 Pour the stock into a saucepan and bring to a boil. Reduce the heat to a gentle simmer.

2 Meanwhile, melt the butter with the oil in a large saucepan and gently fry the garlic, chopped walnuts, and thyme for 2 minutes. Stir in the rice and cook, stirring, for a further 2 minutes until the rice is well-coated in the walnut mixture.

3 Add the stock, ladle by ladle, until all the liquid is absorbed and the rice is thick, creamy, and tender. Keep the heat moderate. This will take about 25 minutes and should not be hurried.

4 Adjust the seasoning and stir in the walnut oil. Serve the risotto sprinkled with the walnut pieces and garnish with thyme.

fragrant herb risotto

USE ANY COMBINATION OF YOUR FAVORITE HERBS IN THIS
RECIPE. THEIR DELICATE FLAVORS ARE ENHANCED BY THE
ADDITION OF WHITE WINE, MAKING THIS THE PERFECT
ACCOMPANIMENT TO A FISH MEAL.

3 3/4 cups (950 mL) vegetable stock

2 Tbsp (25 mL) olive oil

2 medium leeks, trimmed and shredded

2 cups (500 mL) arborio rice

1 1/4 cups (300 mL) dry white wine

Salt and freshly ground black pepper

2 Tbsp (25 mL) each of chopped fresh parsley, sage, basil, marjoram, and tarragon

2 Tbsp (25 mL) sour cream

Mixed fresh herbs, to garnish

1 Pour the stock into a saucepan and bring to a boil. Reduce the heat to a gentle simmer.

2 Meanwhile, heat the oil in a large pan and gently fry the leeks for 2 to 3 minutes until softened but not browned. Add the rice and cook, stirring, for 2 minutes until the rice is well-coated in the leek mixture.

3 Pour in half the wine and cook gently, stirring, until absorbed. Add the remaining wine, and ladle in the stock gradually until all the liquid is absorbed and the rice is thick, creamy, and tender. Keep the heat moderate. This will take about 25 minutes.

4 Season. Stir in the chopped herbs and cream. Garnish and serve.

OPPOSITE FRAGRANT HERB RISOTTO

mixed onion risotto

THIS RISOTTO IS A FLAVORFUL ACCOMPANIMENT TO ROAST MEATS OR ROASTED VEGETABLES.

5 cups (1.25 L) vegetable stock	1 Tbsp (15 mL) lemon juice
¼ cup (50 mL) butter	2 tsp (10 mL) sugar
1 Tbsp (15 mL) vegetable oil	2 cups (500 mL) arborio rice
8 oz (225 g) shallots, halved	⅔ cup (150 mL) dry white wine
2 medium onions, finely sliced	Salt and freshly ground black pepper
2 medium red onions, finely chopped	4 Tbsp (50 mL) snipped fresh chives

1 Pour the stock into a saucepan and bring to a boil. Reduce the heat to a gentle simmer.

2 Meanwhile, melt the butter with the oil in a large saucepan and fry the shallots and onions with the lemon juice and sugar for 8 to 10 minutes until richly golden and caramelized. Stir in the rice and cook, stirring, for a further 2 minutes until well-mixed.

3 Add the wine and cook gently, stirring, until absorbed. Add the stock, ladle by ladle, until all the liquid is absorbed and the rice is thick, creamy, and tender. Keep the heat moderate. This will take about 25 minutes and should not be hurried. Season well. Stir in the chives and serve.

spinach & raisin risotto

SPINACH AND NUTMEG IS A CLASSIC COMBINATION THAT IS IDEAL SERVED AS AN ACCOMPANIMENT TO A RICH MEAT CASSEROLE.

2 lb (1 kg) young spinach leaves, trimmed	1 tsp (5 mL) nutmeg
5 cups (1.25 L) vegetable stock	⅓ cup (90 mL) seedless raisins
¼ cup (50 mL) butter	½ cup (125 mL) toasted pine nuts
1 medium onion, finely chopped	Salt and freshly ground black pepper
2 cups (500 mL) arborio rice	

1 Wash the spinach leaves and place in a large pan while they are still wet. Cover and set over high heat for 4 to 5 minutes until wilted. There will be sufficient water on the spinach from washing to steam the leaves. Reserving any cooking liquid, drain the spinach well, and roughly chop. Set aside.

2 Pour the stock into a saucepan and bring to a boil. Reduce the heat to a gentle simmer.

3 Meanwhile, melt the butter in a large saucepan and gently fry the onion for 2 to 3 minutes until softened but not browned. Stir in the rice and cook, stirring, for 2 minutes until the rice is well-coated in the onion mixture.

4 Add the spinach cooking water to the rice and cook gently, stirring, until absorbed. Add the stock, ladle by ladle, until the liquid is absorbed and the rice thickens and is creamy and tender. Keep the heat moderate. This will take about 25 minutes.

5 Mix in the nutmeg, cooked spinach, raisins, and pine nuts. Season well and serve.

OPPOSITE SPINACH AND RAISIN RISOTTO

four-cheese risotto

THIS DISH USES A RICH COMBINATION OF CREAMY
CHEESES. SERVE AS A MAIN DISH WITH FRESHLY
STEAMED VEGETABLES.

5 cups (1.25 L) vegetable
stock

¼ cup (50 mL) butter

8 oz (225 g) shallots,
finely shredded

2 cups (500 mL) arborio
rice

Salt and freshly ground
black pepper

½ cup (125 mL) freshly
grated Parmesan cheese

⅓ cup (90 mL) coarsely
grated Red Leicester or
mature Cheddar cheese

¼ cup (50 mL) crumbled
Gorgonzola cheese

¼ cup (50 mL) diced
mozzarella cheese

Snipped fresh chives, to
garnish

1 Pour the stock into a saucepan and bring to a boil.
Reduce the heat to a gentle simmer.

2 Meanwhile, melt the butter and gently fry the
shallots for 2 to 3 minutes until softened but not
browned. Stir in the rice and cook, stirring, for 2 minutes,
until the rice is well-coated in the butter.

3 Add a ladleful of stock and cook gently, stirring,
until absorbed. Continue adding the stock, ladle by
ladle, until the mixture becomes thick, creamy, and the
rice is tender. This will take about 25 minutes and should
not be hurried. Season well.

4 Just before serving, gently mix in the cheeses.
Sprinkle with chives and serve immediately, before
the cheeses completely melt.

spinach & gorgonzola risotto

THE DELICATE, EARTHY FLAVOR OF SPINACH COMBINES
PERFECTLY WITH THE RICHNESS OF GORGONZOLA, THE
ITALIAN BLUE CHEESE.

2 lb (1 kg) fresh young
spinach, trimmed

5 cups (1.25 L) vegetable
stock

¼ cup (50 mL) butter

1 bunch scallions, trimmed
and finely chopped

2 cups (500 mL) arborio
rice

Salt and freshly ground
black pepper

¾ cup (200 mL) diced
Gorgonzola cheese

2 Tbsp (25 mL) chopped
fresh chives

Shredded scallion, to
garnish

1 Wash the spinach and place in a large saucepan
while still wet. Cover and cook for 4 to 5 minutes
until wilted. There will be sufficient water on the spinach
from washing to steam the leaves. Reserving any cooking
liquid, drain well, then chop.

2 Pour the stock into a saucepan and bring to a boil.
Reduce the heat to a gentle simmer.

3 Meanwhile, melt the butter in a large saucepan and
gently fry the scallions for 2 to 3 minutes until
softened but not browned. Stir in the rice and cook,
stirring, for 2 minutes until the rice is well-coated in the
onion mixture. Season well.

4 Add the spinach cooking water and cook gently,
stirring, until absorbed. Add the stock ladle by ladle,
until all the liquid is absorbed and the rice is thick,
creamy, and tender. Keep the heat moderate. This will
take about 25 minutes.

5 Stir in the spinach, the Gorgonzola cheese and
chopped chives. Adjust the seasoning if necessary.
Garnish and serve.

OPPOSITE **SPINACH AND GORGONZOLA RISOTTO**

saffron, bell pepper & marsala risotto

THIS COLORFUL AND FRAGRANT RISOTTO HAS THE ADDED SWEETNESS OF BELL PEPPERS AND MARSALA.

2 medium red bell peppers

2 medium yellow bell peppers

2 medium green bell peppers

4 Tbsp (50 mL) Marsala wine

5 cups (1.25 L) vegetable stock

2 Tbsp (25 mL) olive oil

1 medium onion, fine chopped

2 cups (500 mL) arborio rice

Large pinch saffron

Salt and freshly ground black pepper

1 Preheat the broiler to a hot setting. Halve and seed the bell peppers and place on the broiler rack. Cook for 7 to 8 minutes, turning occasionally, until the peppers are charred and softened. Steam the peppers in a plastic bag for about 10 minutes to aid peeling. Carefully peel off the charred skin, then slice the peppers into thin strips. Place in a shallow bowl and mix in the Marsala. Set aside.

2 Pour the stock into a saucepan and bring to a boil. Reduce the heat to a gentle simmer.

3 Meanwhile, heat the oil in a large saucepan and gently fry the onion for 2 to 3 minutes until just softened, but not browned. Add the rice and cook, stirring, for 2 minutes until coated in the onion mixture.

4 Add a ladleful of stock and cook gently, stirring, until absorbed. Continue adding the stock , ladle by ladle, until half the stock is used and the rice becomes creamy. Sprinkle in the saffron and seasoning.

5 Continue adding the stock until the risotto becomes thick and the rice is tender. This will take about 25 minutes and should not be hurried.

6 Stir in the bell pepper mixture and adjust the seasoning before serving.

red onion tomato risotto

FOR A SUBSTANTIAL LUNCH OR DINNER, SERVE THIS FLAVORFUL RISOTTO WITH FRESH CRUSTY BREAD
AND A GREEN SALAD.

½ cup (125 mL) soaked sun-dried tomatoes

4 oz (125 g) cherry tomatoes, halved

3¾ cups (950 mL) vegetable stock

¼ cup (50 mL) butter

2 medium red onions, finely chopped

2 cloves garlic, minced

1 Tbsp (15 mL) lemon juice

2 cups (500 mL) arborio rice

1 tsp (5 mL) dried or 4 tsp (20mL) fresh mixed herbs

Salt and freshly ground black pepper

⅔ cup (150 mL) dry white wine

14-fl oz (398-mL) can chopped tomatoes

1 Tbsp (15 mL) tomato paste

1 tsp (5 mL) sugar

2 Tbsp (25 mL) chopped fresh parsley

1 Reserving the liquid, drain the sun-dried tomatoes. Slice into thin strips. Preheat the broiler to a hot setting and cook the cherry tomatoes for 1 to 2 minutes until lightly charred. Set aside.

2 Pour the stock into a saucepan and bring to a boil. Reduce the heat to a gentle simmer.

3 Meanwhile, melt the butter and gently fry the onion, garlic, lemon juice, and sun-dried tomatoes for 2 to 3 minutes until just softened but not browned. Add the rice and cook, stirring, for 2 minutes until well-mixed. Add the herbs and season.

4 Add the wine, chopped tomatoes, tomato paste, and sugar, and cook gently, stirring, until absorbed. Ladle in the stock gradually until it is all absorbed and the rice is thick, creamy, and tender. Adjust the seasoning if necessary.

5 Gently stir in the broiled cherry tomatoes and serve sprinkled with chopped parsley.

mixed vegetable & bean risotto

THIS HEARTY RISOTTO IS PERFECT COMFORT FOOD ON A COLD DAY.

¾ cup (200 mL) trimmed and halved green beans

2 cups (500 mL) shredded green cabbage

5 cups (1.25 L) vegetable stock (see method)

¼ cup (50 mL) butter

1 large onion, finely chopped

1 clove garlic, minced

2 carrots, peeled and diced

2 sticks celery, trimmed and diced

2 cups (500 mL) arborio rice

14-oz (400-g) can baby lima or white kidney beans, rinsed and drained

7-fl oz (200-mL) can chopped tomatoes

Salt and freshly ground black pepper

1 Tbsp (15 mL) chopped fresh parsley

Parmesan shavings, to garnish

1 Bring a saucepan of water to a boil and cook the green beans for 3 to 4 minutes until tender; cook the cabbage for 2 to 3 minutes until tender. Reserving the cooking liquid, drain the vegetables and set aside. Use the liquid to make up the stock.

2 Pour the stock into a saucepan and bring to a boil. Reduce the heat to a gentle simmer.

3 Meanwhile, melt the butter in a large saucepan and gently fry the onion, garlic, carrot, and celery for 2 to 3 minutes until softened but not browned. Add the rice and cook, stirring, for 2 minutes until the rice is well coated in the vegetable mixture.

4 Add a ladleful of stock and cook gently, stirring until absorbed. Continue adding the stock, ladle by ladle, until it is all absorbed and the rice is thick, creamy, and tender. This takes about 25 minutes and should not be hurried.

5 Stir in the cooked vegetables, beans, and tomatoes, and season well. Heat through, stirring occasionally, for 3 to 4 minutes until hot. Serve sprinkled with parsley and Parmesan shavings.

pilaf-style risotto

THE WARM, SPICY-SWEET MIDDLE EASTERN FLAVORS IN
THIS RISOTTO OFFER THE PERFECT ACCOMPANIMENT TO A
RICH MEAT DISH.

5 cups (1.25 L) vegetable
stock

1 Tbsp (15 mL) olive oil

2 Tbsp (25 mL) butter

1 medium red onion, finely
chopped

1 Tbsp (15 mL) lemon
juice

½ cup (125 mL) thinly
sliced ready-to-eat dried
apricots

1 cinnamon stick, broken

2 cups (500 mL) arborio
rice

Large pinch saffron

Salt and freshly ground
black pepper

3 Tbsp (45 mL) chopped
fresh cilantro

2 Tbsp (25 mL) roasted
pine nuts

2 Tbsp (25 mL) sliced
roasted blanched
almonds

Fresh cilantro, to garnish

1 Pour the stock into a saucepan and bring to a boil.
Reduce the heat to a gentle simmer.

2 Meanwhile, heat the oil and butter in a large
saucepan and gently fry the onion, lemon juice,
apricots, and cinnamon stick for 2 to 3 minutes until the
onion is softened but not browned. Add the rice and
cook, stirring, for 2 minutes until well mixed.

3 Add a ladleful of stock and cook gently, stirring,
until absorbed. Continue adding the stock, ladle by
ladle, until half the stock is used and the rice becomes
creamy. Sprinkle in the saffron and seasoning.

4 Continue adding the stock until the risotto is
creamy. This will take about 25 minutes and should
not be hurried. Remove and discard the cinnamon stick.

5 Mix in the chopped cilantro and adjust the
seasoning if necessary. Serve the risotto sprinkled
with the roasted nuts and garnished with cilantro.

OPPOSITE **PILAF-STYLE RISOTTO**

risotto con vermicelli

AN UNUSUAL DISH COMBINING RICE, PASTA, AND CREAM
CHEESE. THIS NEEDS NO MORE THAN A CRISP SALAD TO
MAKE A FILLING MEAL.

4 oz (125 mL) tricolor
vermicelli or spaghetti,
broken into short
lengths

1 Tbsp (15 mL) olive oil

5 cups (1.25 L) vegetable
stock

¼ cup (50 mL) butter

1 medium onion, finely
chopped

1 clove garlic, minced

2 cups (500 mL) arborio
rice

½ cup (125 mL) garlic and
herb-flavored soft
cheese

4 Tbsp (50 mL) heavy
cream

Salt and freshly ground
black pepper

3 Tbsp (45 mL) chopped
fresh parsley

1-oz (25-g) piece
Parmesan cheese

1 Bring a saucepan of water to a boil and cook the
pasta according to the package instructions. Drain
well and toss immediately with the olive oil. Set aside.

2 Pour the stock into a saucepan and bring to a boil.
Reduce the heat to a gentle simmer.

3 Meanwhile, melt the butter and gently fry the onion
and garlic for 2 to 3 minutes until just softened but
not browned. Add the rice and cook, stirring, for 2 minutes
until well-coated in the onion butter.

4 Add the stock, ladle by ladle, until all the liquid
has been absorbed, and the rice is thick, creamy,
and tender. Keep the heat moderate. This will take about
25 minutes.

5 Carefully mix in the cooked pasta, soft cheese,
cream, and seasoning. Stir in the parsley. Transfer
to a serving dish. Garnish with Parmesan shavings.

chili bean risotto

PACKED FULL OF THE FLAVORS OF MEXICO, THIS VIBRANT RISOTTO MAKES A SUBSTANTIAL MAIN MEAL SERVED ON ITS OWN.

5 cups (1.25 L) vegetable stock

2 Tbsp (25 mL) vegetable oil

1 large onion, finely chopped

1 clove garlic, minced

1 green chile, seeded and finely chopped

2 green bell peppers, seeded and diced

2 cups (500 mL) arborio rice

1 tsp (5 mL) ground cumin

1 tsp (5 mL) ground coriander

1 tsp (5 mL) chili powder

Salt and freshly ground black pepper

14-oz (400-g) can kidney beans, drained and rinsed

12-oz (350-g) can corn, drained and rinsed

4 medium tomatoes, peeled, seeded, and chopped

1 Pour the stock into a saucepan and bring to a boil. Reduce the heat to a gentle simmer.

2 Meanwhile, heat the oil in a large saucepan and gently fry the onion, garlic, chile, and bell peppers for 4 to 5 minutes until softened, but not browned. Stir in the rice and cook, stirring, for 2 minutes until the rice is coated in the vegetable mixture.

3 Add a ladleful of stock and cook gently, stirring, until absorbed. Continue adding the stock ladle by ladle until half the stock is used. Stir in the spices, seasoning, and kidney beans.

4 Continue adding the stock until the risotto is thick, but not sticky. This will take about 25 minutes and should not be hurried.

5 Stir in the corn and tomatoes. Mix well, adjust seasoning if necessary, and serve.

oriental vegetable risotto

TRY SERVING THIS COMBINATION OF RICE AND STIR-FRIED VEGETABLES AS AN ACCOMPANIMENT TO A CHINESE MEAL. ITS DELICATE FLAVORS ARE PERFECT TO SERVE WITH FISH OR POULTRY.

2 Tbsp (25 mL) vegetable oil

1 bunch scallions, trimmed and chopped

1 medium red bell pepper, seeded and sliced

1 medium yellow bell pepper, seeded and sliced

4 oz (125 g) snow peas, trimmed

4 oz (125 g) oyster mushrooms

2 oz (50 g) bean sprouts

2 Tbsp (25 mL) dark soy sauce

5 cups (1.25 L) vegetable stock

2 cloves garlic, finely chopped

1-in (2.5-cm) piece fresh ginger, grated

2 cups (500 mL) arborio rice

1 tsp (5 mL) Chinese 5-spice powder

2 tsp (10 mL) sesame oil

Salt and white pepper

1 Tbsp (15 mL) toasted sesame seeds

1 Heat 1 Tbsp (15 mL) oil in a wok or large skillet and stir-fry the scallions, bell peppers, and snow peas over high heat for 2 minutes. Add the oyster mushrooms, bean sprouts, and soy sauce, and stir-fry for a further 1 minute. Set aside.

2 Pour the stock into a saucepan and bring to a boil. Reduce the heat to a gentle simmer.

3 Meanwhile, heat the remaining oil in a large saucepan and gently fry the garlic and ginger for 1 to 2 minutes until softened. Add the rice and cook, stirring, for 2 minutes until the rice is well coated.

4 Add the stock, ladle by ladle, until the stock is absorbed and the rice is thick, creamy, and tender. Keep the heat moderate. This will take about 25 minutes. Stir in the 5-spice powder.

5 Fold in the stir-fried vegetables and sesame oil. Heat gently for 1 to 2 minutes until hot. Taste and season. Serve sprinkled with sesame seeds.

RISOTTO WITH MEAT

Risotto with Coriander Meatballs

Raspberry Lamb Risotto

Risotto della Carni

Char-grilled Pork with Mixed Bell Pepper Risotto

Bacon and Spinach Risotto

Sweet Chili and Basil Risotto

Beef Ragù Risotto

Hot Chili Risotto

Rosemary Lamb Risotto

Risotto alla Bolognese

Basil and Pork Saffron Risotto

Fried Lamb and Fava Bean Risotto

Beef and Olive Risotto

Ham and Bean Risotto

Leek and Artichoke Ham Risotto

Beef and Broccoli Risotto

Ham and Mixed Mushroom Risotto

Persian Lamb Risotto

risotto with coriander meatballs

THE SPICY MEATBALLS ARE COOKED SEPARATELY FROM THE MAIN RISOTTO AND SERVED ON TOP OF THE RICE. THIS NEEDS ONLY A GREEN SALAD FOR A COMPLETE MEAL.

FOR THE MEATBALLS

1 cup (250 mL) ground lamb

1 onion, finely chopped

1 clove garlic, minced

1 stick celery, finely chopped

1 tsp (5 mL) ground cumin

1 tsp (5 mL) ground coriander

2 Tbsp (25 mL) dried apricots soaked for 30 minutes and finely chopped

Salt and freshly ground black pepper

1 Tbsp (15 mL) clear honey

2 Tbsp (25 mL) butter

1 Tbsp (15 mL) oil

FOR THE RISOTTO

5 cups (1.25 L) lamb stock

¼ cup (50 mL) butter

1 onion, finely chopped

2 cloves garlic, minced

2 cups (500 mL) arborio rice

Salt and freshly ground black pepper

1 tsp (5 mL) coriander seeds, crushed

4 Tbsp (50 mL) chopped fresh cilantro

1 Place the ground lamb, onion, garlic, celery, cumin, coriander, apricots, seasoning, and honey in a mixing bowl and mix together. Roll into 8 equal-sized balls and reserve.

2 Meanwhile, pour the lamb stock into a saucepan and bring to a boil. Reduce the heat to a gentle simmer.

3 Melt the butter in a large skillet and gently cook the onion and garlic for 2 minutes until the onion has softened but not browned. Stir in the rice and cook for a further 2 minutes until the rice is well-coated in butter.

4 Add a ladleful of stock to the rice and cook, stirring, until the liquid has been absorbed. Continue adding the stock in small quantities until half of the stock has been used and the rice is creamy. Season well and add the coriander seeds.

5 Continue adding the stock until the risotto is thick but not sticky. This will take about 25 minutes.

6 Meanwhile, melt the butter with the oil in a separate pan and cook the meatballs for 10 to 15 minutes, turning, until browned and done. Drain and keep warm.

7 Stir the cilantro into the risotto and transfer to a warmed serving bowl. Arrange the meatballs on top and serve.

raspberry lamb risotto

FRUIT IS A PERFECT ACCOMPANIMENT TO LAMB AS IT COUNTERS SOME OF THE MEAT'S FATTINESS. RASPBERRIES ADD VIBRANT COLOR AS WELL AS A SLIGHTLY TART FLAVOR TO THIS DISH.

5 cups (1.25 L) lamb stock

1/4 cup (50 mL) butter

2 cups (500 mL) trimmed and cubed lean lamb

1 red onion, cut into eight

3 cloves garlic, minced

2 cups (500 mL) arborio rice

Salt and freshly ground black pepper

2 Tbsp (25 mL) raspberry vinegar

2 Tbsp (25 mL) clear honey

2 cups (500 mL) shredded red cabbage

1 cup (250 mL) raspberries

1 tsp (5 mL) poppy seeds

1 Pour the stock into a saucepan and bring to a boil. Reduce the heat to a gentle simmer.

2 Meanwhile, melt the butter in a large skillet and gently cook the lamb for 2 to 3 minutes until sealed. Add the onion and garlic and cook, stirring, for 2 minutes until the onion has softened but not browned. Stir in the rice and cook for a further 2 minutes, stirring, until the rice is well-coated in butter.

3 Add a ladleful of the stock and cook gently, stirring until the liquid has been absorbed. Continue adding stock until half of the stock has been used and the rice is creamy. Season well and add the raspberry vinegar, honey, and red cabbage.

4 Continue adding the stock to the rice until the risotto is thick but not sticky, about 25 minutes. Stir in the raspberries, garnish with poppy seeds and serve in a warm bowl.

risotto della carni

THIS RECIPE USES ONE OF THE BEST LOVED ITALIAN MEATS, PROSCIUTTO. IT HAS A DELICATE FLAVOR AND IS PERFECT WITH THE PORK AND GARLIC-FLAVORED MORTADELLA SAUSAGE.

3 3/4 cups (950 mL) pork, veal or vegetable stock

1 1/4 cups (300 mL) dry white wine

1/4 cup (50 mL) butter

1 1/4 cups (300 mL) trimmed and cubed lean pork

1 onion, finely chopped

2 cloves garlic, sliced

2 cups (500 mL) arborio rice

Salt and freshly ground black pepper

1/3 cup (90 mL) prosciutto, shredded

3/4 cup (200 mL) quartered mortadella slices

12 sun-dried tomatoes in oil, drained and shredded

2 Tbsp (25 mL) chopped fresh basil

2 Tbsp (25 mL) freshly grated Parmesan cheese

1 Pour the stock and wine into a pan and bring to a boil. Reduce the heat to a gentle simmer.

2 Meanwhile, melt the butter in a large skillet and gently cook the pork for 2 minutes until sealed. Add the onion and garlic and cook, stirring, until the onion has softened but not browned. Stir in the rice and cook for 2 minutes, stirring, until the rice is well-coated.

3 Add a ladleful of stock and cook gently until the liquid has been absorbed. Continue to add small quantities of stock until half of the stock has been used and the rice is creamy. Season well.

4 Continue adding the stock for 20 minutes. Stir in the prosciutto and mortadella, sun-dried tomatoes, and basil. Cook for a further 5 minutes until the risotto is thick but not sticky. Just before serving, stir in the cheese and serve in a warmed bowl.

char-grilled pork
with mixed bell
pepper risotto

TENDER PORK IS MARINATED IN A SPICY MARINADE
THEN BROILED, ADDING A SMOKY FLAVOR AND COLOR
TO THIS RISOTTO.

12-oz (350-g) piece lean
pork fillet, halved
lengthwise

2 Tbsp (25 mL) dark soy
sauce

2 Tbsp (25 mL) red wine

1 Tbsp (15 mL) liquid
honey

1 Tbsp (15 mL) dark
brown sugar

2 cloves garlic, minced

½ tsp (2 mL) ground
cinnamon

1 tsp (5 mL) sesame oil

FOR THE RISOTTO

5 cups (1.25 L) pork or
vegetable stock

¼ cup (50 mL) butter

1 leek, sliced

2 cloves garlic, minced

2 cups (500 mL) arborio
rice

1 red bell pepper, seeded
and chopped

1 green bell pepper,
seeded and chopped

1 yellow bell pepper,
seeded and chopped

2 tsp (10 mL) fennel seeds

1 Put the pork pieces in a shallow dish. Mix together
the soy sauce, red wine, honey, brown sugar, garlic,
cinnamon, and sesame oil. Pour the mixture over the pork,
turning to coat completely. Leave for a few minutes.
Meanwhile heat the broiler to medium and cook the pork
for 20 minutes or until done. Keep warm.

2 Meanwhile, pour the stock into a large saucepan and
bring to a boil. Reduce the heat to a gentle simmer.
Melt the butter in a large skillet and gently fry the leek
and garlic for 2 to 3 minutes until the leek is softened but
not brown. Stir in the rice and cook for 2 to 3 minutes,
stirring, until well-coated in butter.

3 Add a ladleful of stock and cook gently, stirring until
the liquid has been absorbed. Continue adding
ladlefuls of stock until half of the stock has been used and
the rice is creamy.

4 Continue adding the stock for 10 minutes. Add the
bell peppers and fennel seeds, stirring well. Continue
to cook, adding more stock for a further 15 minutes until
the risotto is thick but not sticky.

5 Remove the pork from the broiler and slice. Stir into
the rice and serve in a warmed bowl.

bacon & spinach risotto

SPINACH AND BACON ARE A CLASSIC COMBINATION. USING SMOKED BACON ADDS FLAVOR THAT PERFECTLY COMPLEMENTS THE SPINACH AND TOMATOES.

5 cups (1.25 L) vegetable stock

¼ cup (50 mL) butter

1 red onion, halved and sliced

2 cloves garlic, minced

1⅓ cups (340 mL) rindless smoked bacon, shredded

2 cups (500 mL) arborio rice

Salt and freshly ground black pepper

Large pinch nutmeg

2 tomatoes, seeded and chopped

6 oz (175 g) spinach, trimmed and washed

½ cup (125 mL) freshly grated Romano cheese

Finely pared zest of 1 lemon

1 Pour the stock into a large saucepan and bring to a boil. Reduce the heat to a gentle simmer.

2 Meanwhile, melt the butter in a large skillet and gently fry the onion, garlic, and bacon for 2 to 3 minutes until the onion has softened but not browned and the bacon is sealed. Stir in the rice and cook, stirring, for 2 minutes until the rice is well-coated.

3 Add a ladleful of stock to the pan and cook gently until absorbed. Continue to add the stock in small quantities until half of it has been used and the rice is creamy. Season well and add the nutmeg and tomatoes.

4 Continue to add the stock until the risotto becomes thick but not sticky, about 25 minutes.

5 Meanwhile, cook the spinach in a large, covered pan for a few minutes. Stir into the risotto 2 to 3 minutes before serving with the cheese and lemon zest.

OPPOSITE BACON AND SPINACH RISOTTO

sweet chili & basil risotto

BASIL HAS A UNIQUE FLAVOR WHICH IS CLOSELY RELATED TO ITS FRAGRANCE. ITS OIL IS VOLATILE AND IS LOST IN COOKING, THEREFORE IT SHOULD ONLY BE ADDED AT THE END OF A RECIPE FOR FULL FLAVOR.

3¾ cups (950 mL) stock of your choice

¼ cup (50 mL) butter

1 Tbsp (15 mL) oil

2 cups (500 mL) lean flank or sirloin steak, trimmed and shredded

2 cloves garlic, minced

2 tsp (10 mL) fresh ginger, chopped

1 tsp (5 mL) chili powder

1 Tbsp (15 mL) dark soy sauce

1 tsp (5 mL) chili sauce

2 Tbsp (25 mL) clear honey

2 cups (500 mL) arborio rice

Freshly ground black pepper

2 red chiles, seeded and sliced

4 scallions, trimmed and sliced

4 Tbsp (50 mL) chopped fresh basil

1 Pour the stock into a saucepan and bring to a boil. Reduce the heat to a gentle simmer.

2 Meanwhile, melt the butter in a large skillet with the oil and gently cook the beef for 2 to 3 minutes until sealed. Stir in the garlic, ginger, chili powder, soy and chili sauces, and honey. Stir in the rice and cook for 2 minutes, stirring, until the rice is well-coated in butter.

3 Add a ladleful of stock to the rice and cook, stirring, until the liquid has been absorbed. Continue to add small quantities of stock to the rice until half of the stock has been used and the rice is creamy. Season with pepper and add the red chiles, mixing well.

4 Continue adding the stock until the risotto is thick but not sticky. This should take about 25 minutes. Just before serving, stir in the scallions and basil. Serve in a warm bowl.

beef ragù risotto

RAGÙ IS A BOLOGNESE SAUCE TYPICALLY SERVED WITH
PASTA. HERE IT MAKES A DELICIOUSLY SATISFYING MEAL.

3³/₄ cups (950 mL) beef stock

1¹/₄ cups (300 mL) red wine

¹/₄ cup (50 mL) butter

1 tsp (5 mL) oil

2 cups (500 mL) trimmed and cubed lean flank or sirloin steak

1 large onion, cut into eight

1 clove garlic, minced

2 cups (500 mL) arborio rice

Salt and freshly ground black pepper

1 carrot, halved and sliced

2 sticks celery, sliced

1 Tbsp (15 mL) tomato paste

2 large tomatoes, seeded and chopped

1 Tbsp (15 mL) chopped oregano

1 Pour the stock and wine into a saucepan and bring to a boil. Reduce the heat to a gentle simmer.

2 Meanwhile melt the butter in a large skillet with the oil and gently fry the beef over medium heat for 3 minutes, stirring, until sealed. Add the onion and garlic and cook for 2 minutes until the onion is softened but not browned. Stir in the rice and cook, stirring, for 2 minutes until the rice is well-coated in butter.

3 Add a ladleful of the stock and wine mixture to the rice and cook gently, stirring, until the liquid has been absorbed. Continue adding small quantities of the stock mixture until half of the stock has been used and the rice is creamy. Season well and add the carrot, celery, tomato paste, and tomatoes.

4 Continue adding the stock mixture until the risotto becomes thick but not sticky, about 25 minutes. Sprinkle in the herbs and serve in a warm bowl with warm crusty bread and a fresh salad of mixed greens.

hot chili risotto

THIS DISH HAS A LOT OF HEAT. IF YOU FIND IT TOO
MUCH TO HANDLE, REDUCE THE NUMBER OF CHILES
OR OMIT THE CHILI POWDER.

3³/₄ cups (950 mL) beef stock

2 Tbsp (25 mL) butter

1 Tbsp (15 mL) oil

2 cups (500 mL) lean flank or sirloin steak, trimmed and cut into 2-in (5-cm) cubes

1 onion, finely chopped

2 cloves garlic, minced

1 tsp (5 mL) chili powder

2 cups (500 mL) arborio rice

2 red chiles, seeded and sliced

One 14-fl oz (398-mL) can chopped tomatoes

1 cup (250 mL) canned red kidney beans, drained

Salt and freshly ground black pepper

1 Tbsp (15 mL) chopped oregano or basil

¹/₄ cup (50 mL) freshly grated mozzarella cheese

1 Pour the stock into a saucepan and bring to a boil. Reduce the heat to a gentle simmer.

2 Meanwhile, melt the butter with the oil in a large skillet. Gently cook the beef for 3 to 4 minutes until sealed. Add the onion, garlic, and chili powder and cook for 2 to 3 minutes until the onion has softened but not browned. Stir in the rice and cook for 2 minutes, stirring, until the rice is well-coated in butter.

3 Add a ladleful of stock and cook gently, stirring, until the liquid has been absorbed. Continue adding small quantities of the stock until half of the stock has been used and the rice is creamy. Add the chiles, tomatoes, kidney beans, and seasoning.

4 Continue adding the stock until the risotto is thick but not sticky, about 25 minutes.

5 Just before serving, stir in the herbs and add the mozzarella cheese. Serve in a warm bowl.

OPPOSITE **HOT CHILI RISOTTO**

rosemary lamb risotto

ROSEMARY HAS A POWERFUL FLAVOR AND SHOULD BE USED IN MODERATION. UNLIKE OTHER HERBS IT WILL WITHSTAND
COOKING AND IS USUALLY USED IN COMBINATION WITH LAMB.

4 cups (1 L) lamb stock

⅔ cup (150 mL) rosé wine

¼ cup (50 mL) butter

1 Tbsp (15 mL) olive oil

2 cups (500 mL) cubed lean lamb

1 onion, cut into eight

2 cloves garlic, sliced

2 cups (500 mL) arborio rice

1 yellow bell pepper, seeded and chopped

1 green bell pepper, seeded and chopped

2 sprigs rosemary

2 tsp (10 mL) cumin seeds, roughly crushed

Salt and freshly ground black pepper

1 Tbsp (15 mL) tomato paste

Sprigs fresh rosemary

1 Pour the stock and wine into a saucepan and bring to a boil. Reduce the heat to a gentle simmer.

2 Meanwhile, melt the butter in a large skillet with the olive oil and gently fry the lamb for 2 to 3 minutes until sealed. Add the onion and garlic and cook, stirring, for 2 minutes until the onion has softened but not browned. Stir in the rice and cook, stirring, for 2 minutes until the rice is well-coated.

3 Add a ladleful of stock and wine mixture and cook gently, stirring, until the liquid has been absorbed. Continue to add small quantities of stock mixture until half of the liquid has been used and the rice is creamy. Add the bell peppers, rosemary, and cumin seeds and season well. Mix the tomato paste with a little of the hot stock and stir into the rice.

4 Continue adding the stock mixture until the risotto becomes thick but not sticky, about 25 minutes. Just before serving, remove the rosemary sprigs from the risotto and replace with fresh rosemary. Serve in a warm bowl.

risotto alla bolognese

USUALLY ASSOCIATED WITH SPAGHETTI, THE RICH SAUCE
FLAVORING THIS RISOTTO CONTAINS ALL THE CLASSIC
BOLOGNESE INGREDIENTS.

**3¾ cups (950 mL) beef
stock**

⅔ cup (150 mL) red wine

¼ cup (50 mL) butter

**1 cup (250 mL) ground
beef or veal**

**2 rindless bacon slices,
chopped**

1 onion, finely chopped

2 cloves garlic, minced

**2 cups (500 mL) arborio
rice**

**Salt and freshly ground
black pepper**

**2 Tbsp (25 mL) tomato
paste**

**7-fl oz (200-mL) can
chopped tomatoes**

1 carrot, diced

1 stick celery, sliced

**2 Tbsp (25 mL) chopped
fresh oregano**

1 Pour the stock and wine into a saucepan and bring
to a boil. Reduce the heat to a gentle simmer.

2 Meanwhile, melt the butter in a large skillet and
gently cook the ground beef and bacon for 2 to
3 minutes until the beef is sealed. Add the onion and
garlic and cook for a further 2 minutes, stirring, until
the onion has softened but not browned. Stir in the rice
and cook for 2 minutes, stirring, until the rice is well-
coated in butter.

3 Add a ladleful of stock and wine and cook gently,
stirring, until the liquid has been absorbed.
Continue adding stock until half of the stock has been
used and the rice is creamy. Season well and stir in the
tomato paste, tomatoes, carrot, and celery.

4 Continue adding the stock until the risotto becomes
thick but not sticky, about 25 minutes. Stir in the
oregano and serve in a warmed bowl.

basil & pork saffron risotto

SAFFRON GIVES THE RICE IN THIS RECIPE A DELICATE
YELLOW COLOR AND BITTERSWEET FLAVOR. SAFFRON IS
WIDELY USED IN RICE DISHES AROUND THE WORLD.

**5 cups (1.25 L) pork or
vegetable stock**

¼ cup (50 mL) butter

**2 cups (500 mL) lean
pork, trimmed and
shredded**

1 onion, finely chopped

2 cloves garlic, minced

**2 cups (500 mL) arborio
rice**

Large pinch saffron

**Salt and freshly ground
black pepper**

**4 oz (125 g) baby corn,
sliced**

**4 oz (125 g) green beans,
trimmed**

**4 Tbsp (50 mL) chopped
fresh basil**

1 Tbsp (15 mL) pine nuts

**2 Tbsp (25 mL) freshly
grated Romano cheese**

1 Pour the stock into a saucepan and bring to a boil.
Reduce the heat to a gentle simmer.

2 Meanwhile, melt the butter in a large saucepan and
gently fry the pork for 2 minutes until sealed. Add
the onion and garlic and cook for 2 minutes until the
onion is softened but not browned. Stir in the rice and
cook, stirring, for a further 2 minutes until the rice is
well-coated in butter.

3 Add a ladleful of stock and cook gently until
absorbed. Continue to add small quantities of stock
until half of the stock has been used and the rice is
creamy. Stir in the saffron, seasoning, corn, and beans.

4 Continue adding stock until the risotto is thick but
not sticky, about 25 minutes. Stir in the basil, pine
nuts, and cheese, serve in a warm bowl.

OPPOSITE **BASIL AND PORK SAFFRON RISOTTO**

fried lamb & fava bean risotto

TURMERIC IS USED IN THIS RECIPE TO DELICATELY COLOR AND FLAVOR THE RICE, COMPLEMENTING THE GREEN COLOR OF THE BEANS PERFECTLY. TURMERIC IS A MEMBER OF THE GINGER FAMILY AND HAS A PUNGENT FLAVOR AND WOODY AROMA.

3¾ cups (950 mL) lamb stock

1¼ cups (300 mL) dry white wine

¼ cup (50 mL) butter

2 cups (500 mL) trimmed and cubed lean lamb

1 onion, finely chopped

2 cloves garlic, minced

2 cups (500 mL) arborio rice

Juice of 1 lemon

1 Tbsp (15 mL) brown sugar

Pinch turmeric

Salt and freshly ground black pepper

1 tsp (5 mL) paprika

4 oz (125 g) shelled fava beans, thawed if frozen

2 Tbsp (25 mL) freshly grated Romano cheese

1 Pour the stock and wine into a saucepan and bring to a boil. Reduce the heat to a gentle simmer.

2 Meanwhile, melt the butter in a large skillet and cook the lamb gently for 2 to 3 minutes, stirring, until sealed. Add the onion and garlic and cook for a further 2 minutes until the onion has softened but not browned. Stir in the rice, lemon, sugar, and turmeric and cook for 2 minutes, stirring, until the rice is well-coated in butter.

3 Add a ladleful of the stock to the rice and cook, stirring, until the liquid has been absorbed. Continue adding small quantities of stock to the rice until half of the stock has been used and the rice is creamy. Season well and add the paprika.

4 Cook the fava beans in boiling water for 5 minutes and drain well. Meanwhile, continue adding stock to the rice until the risotto is thick but not sticky, about 25 minutes. Just before serving, stir in the beans and cheese.

beef & olive risotto

TRY TO USE GOOD-QUALITY OLIVES WHICH HAVE BEEN MARINATED IN GARLIC AND SPICES TO ADD EXTRA FLAVOR TO THIS RECIPE.

¼ cup (50 mL) dried porcini mushrooms

5 cups (1.25 L) beef stock

¼ cup (50 mL) butter

1 Tbsp (15 mL) oil

2 cups (500 mL) lean flank or sirloin steak, trimmed and shredded

2 leeks, sliced

3 cloves garlic, minced

2 cups (500 mL) arborio rice

Salt and freshly ground black pepper

½ cup (125 mL) garlic-marinated black olives, drained, pitted, and halved

½ cup (125 mL) marinated green olives, drained, pitted, and halved

¼ cup (50 mL) pimento in oil, drained and shredded

¼ cup (50 mL) walnut halves

2 Tbsp (25 mL) chopped fresh mixed herbs such as basil, thyme, oregano, and parsley

1 Soak the porcini mushrooms in warm water according to the instructions on the package. Drain and slice. Pour the stock into a saucepan and bring to a boil. Reduce the heat to a gentle simmer.

2 Meanwhile, melt the butter in a large skillet with the oil and gently fry the beef for 2 to 3 minutes until sealed. Add the leeks and garlic and cook, stirring, for 2 minutes. Stir in the rice and cook for a further 2 minutes, stirring, until the rice is well-coated in butter.

3 Add a ladleful of stock to the rice and cook, stirring until the liquid has been absorbed. Continue to add small quantities of stock to the rice until half of the stock has been used and the rice is creamy. Season well and stir in the olives, mushrooms, pimento, and walnuts.

4 Continue to add the stock to the pan until the risotto is thick but not sticky, about 25 minutes. Stir in the herbs, adjust the seasoning and serve in a warm bowl with ciabatta or other crusty bread.

ham & bean risotto

SMOKED HAM GIVES A RICH FLAVOR TO THIS DISH. COMBINED WITH THE BEANS, WINE, AND FRESH HERBS, IT IS A SIMPLE HEARTY DISH.

3¾ cups (950 mL) vegetable stock

1¼ cups (300 mL) dry white wine

¼ cup (90 mL) butter

1 red onion, finely chopped

1 clove garlic, minced

1½ cups (375 mL) diced smoked ham

2 cups (500 mL) arborio rice

Salt and freshly ground black pepper

Pinch turmeric

4 oz (125 g) shelled fava beans, thawed if frozen

4 oz (125 g) thin green beans, trimmed

4 oz (125 g) canned baby lima beans, drained

½ cup (125 mL) freshly grated Romano cheese

1 Tbsp (15 mL) chopped fresh sage

1 Pour the stock and wine into a large pan and bring to a boil. Reduce the heat to a gentle simmer.

2 Meanwhile, melt the butter in a large skillet and gently fry the onion, garlic, and ham for 2 to 3 minutes until the onion is softened but not browned. Stir in the rice and cook, stirring, for 2 to 3 minutes until the rice is well-coated in butter.

3 Add a ladleful of stock to the rice, cook gently, stirring, until the liquid has been absorbed. Continue to add ladlefuls of stock to the rice until half of the stock has been used and the rice is creamy. Season well and add the turmeric.

4 Continue adding stock until the risotto becomes thick but not sticky, about 25 minutes.

5 Meanwhile, cook the fava (broad) beans and green beans in boiling water for 5 minutes. Five minutes before the end of the risotto cooking time, add the boiled beans and canned baby lima beans. Stir in the cheese and sage, and serve in a warmed bowl.

OPPOSITE **HAM AND BEAN RISOTTO**

leek & artichoke ham risotto

HAM AND LEEKS ARE A GREAT COMBINATION, ESPECIALLY WHEN ENHANCED BY GRAINY MUSTARD. FOR VARIETY, ONE OF THE MANY FLAVORED MUSTARDS NOW AVAILABLE COULD BE ADDED.

5 cups (1.25 L) vegetable or pork stock

¼ cup (50 mL) butter

3 large leeks, sliced

2 cloves garlic, minced

1⅓ cups (340 mL) ham, trimmed and cut into strips

2 cups (500 mL) arborio rice

1 Tbsp (15 mL) whole-grain mustard

Salt and freshly ground black pepper

8 canned artichoke hearts, drained and halved

½ cup (125 mL) freshly grated Parmesan cheese

1 Tbsp (15 mL) chopped fresh cilantro

1 Pour the stock into a large saucepan and bring to a boil. Reduce the heat to a gentle simmer.

2 Meanwhile, melt the butter in a large skillet and gently fry the leeks, garlic, and ham slices for 2 to 3 minutes until the leeks have softened. Stir in the rice and cook, stirring, for 2 minutes until the rice is well-coated in butter.

3 Add a ladleful of the stock and cook gently, stirring, until the liquid has been absorbed. Continue to add ladlefuls of stock to the rice until half of the stock has been used and the rice is creamy. Stir in the mustard and season well.

4 Continue adding the stock until the risotto is thick but not sticky, about 25 minutes. Stir in the artichoke hearts 2 to 3 minutes before the end of the cooking time. Add the cheese and cilantro and serve in a warmed bowl.

OPPOSITE **LEEK AND ARTICHOKE HAM RISOTTO**

beef & broccoli risotto

BEEF AND BROCCOLI ARE WIDELY USED IN CHINESE COOKERY. IN THIS RECIPE, SOY SAUCE, SHERRY, SUGAR, AND FENNEL ARE USED TO GIVE A SUBTLE ORIENTAL FLAVOR.

5 cups (1.25 L) beef stock

¼ cup (50 mL) butter

2 cups (500 mL) lean flank or sirloin steak, trimmed and shredded

1 onion, halved and sliced

2 cloves garlic, minced

3 Tbsp (45 mL) light soy sauce

2 Tbsp (25 mL) dry sherry

1 tsp (5 mL) brown sugar

¼ cup (50 mL) blanched almonds

2 cups (500 mL) arborio rice

Freshly ground black pepper

2 tsp (10 mL) fennel seeds

6 oz (175 g) broccoli florets

2 Tbsp (25 mL) freshly grated Parmesan cheese

1 Pour the stock into a saucepan and bring to a boil. Reduce the heat to a gentle simmer.

2 Meanwhile, melt the butter in a large skillet and sauté the beef for 2 minutes until sealed. Add the onion and garlic and cook, stirring, for 2 minutes until the onion has softened but not browned. Stir in the soy sauce, sherry, sugar, and almonds and cook for 2 minutes. Stir in the rice and cook, stirring, for a further 2 minutes until the rice is well-coated in butter.

3 Add a ladleful of stock and cook, stirring, until the liquid has been absorbed. Continue to add small quantities of the stock until half of the stock has been used and the rice is creamy. Season well with pepper and add the fennel seeds.

4 Continue adding the stock until the risotto is thick but not sticky, about 25 minutes. Meanwhile cook the broccoli in boiling water for 5 minutes, then drain well. Stir the broccoli and cheese into the risotto and serve in a warm bowl.

ham & mixed mushroom risotto

PORCINI MUSHROOMS ARE MUCH SOUGHT FOR THEIR EARTHY, NUTTY FLAVOR. THEY ARE AVAILABLE DRIED, AND ARE SIMPLY SOFTENED IN HOT WATER FOR USE IN SMALL QUANTITIES IN MANY CLASSIC RECIPES.

¼ cup (50 mL) dried porcini mushrooms

3 cups (750 mL) vegetable stock

1¼ cups (300 mL) dry white wine

⅓ cup (90 mL) butter

1 onion, finely chopped

3 cloves garlic, minced

2¼ cups (550 mL) wild mushrooms of your choice, wiped and sliced

2¼ cups (550 mL) baby button mushrooms, wiped

2 cups (500 mL) arborio rice

Salt and freshly ground black pepper

1½ cups (300 mL) oyster mushrooms

½ cup (125 mL) Parma ham, shredded

1 Tbsp (15 mL) chopped fresh parsley or thyme

2 Tbsp (25 mL) freshly grated Parmesan cheese

1 Soak the porcini mushrooms in warm water according to the instructions on the package then thinly slice. Reserve the soaking liquid.

2 Pour the stock and wine into a large saucepan and bring to a boil. Reduce the heat to a gentle simmer.

3 Meanwhile, melt the butter in a large skillet and gently fry the onion and garlic for 2 to 3 minutes until softened but not browned. Add all the mushrooms except the oyster mushrooms and cook for a further 2 minutes, stirring.

4 Add the rice and porcini with soaking liquid, stirring, until the liquid has been absorbed. Stir in a ladleful of stock and wine mixture. Cook gently until absorbed and continue to add ladlefuls of stock until half of the stock has been used and the rice is creamy. Season well.

5 Continue to add the stock in small quantities until the risotto becomes thick but not sticky, about 25 minutes. 5 minutes before the end of the cooking time, stir in the oyster mushrooms and Parma ham.

6 Just before serving, stir in the herbs and cheese, adjust seasoning, and serve in a warm bowl.

persian lamb risotto

CILANTRO, FRUIT, AND CINNAMON ARE CLASSIC FLAVORINGS IN PERSIAN RECIPES AND MAKE PERFECT PARTNERS FOR LAMB.

¼ cup (50 mL) dried apricots

3¾ cups (950 mL) lamb stock

1¼ cups (300 mL) dry white wine

¼ cup (50 mL) butter

2 cups (500 mL) trimmed and cubed lean lamb

1 red onion, halved and sliced

3 cloves garlic, minced

1 tsp (5 mL) fresh ginger, chopped

1 tsp (5 mL) ground allspice

1 tsp (5 mL) ground cinnamon

1 tsp (5 mL) ground cumin

2 cups (500 mL) arborio rice

Freshly ground black pepper

¼ cup (50 mL) shelled walnut halves

2 Tbsp (25 mL) chopped fresh cilantro

1 Soak the apricots in warm water for 30 minutes. Reserving the liquid, drain and chop the apricots. Set aside. Add the liquid to the stock and wine and pour into a saucepan. Bring to a boil, then reduce the heat to a gentle simmer.

2 Meanwhile, melt the butter in a large skillet and gently fry the lamb for 2 to 3 minutes until sealed. Add the onion and garlic and cook for 2 minutes until the onion is softened but not browned. Stir in the spices and cook 1 minute, stirring.

3 Add the rice and cook for 2 minutes, stirring, until the rice is well-coated in butter. Add a ladleful of the stock and cook, stirring, until the liquid is absorbed. Continue to add small quantities of the stock to the rice until half of the stock has been used and the rice is creamy. Season well with pepper.

4 Continue adding the stock until the risotto is thick but not sticky, about 25 minutes. Stir in the apricots, walnuts, and cilantro and serve in a warm bowl with hot bread.

RISOTTO WITH POULTRY

Chicken and Corn Risotto with Croutons

Chicken and Tarragon Mushroom Risotto

Smoked Chicken and Mango Risotto

Chicken Asparagus Risotto

Chicken and Artichoke Risotto

Risotto alla Cacciatore

Chicken with Caramelized Apple and
Brandy Risotto

Risotto Coq au Vin

Lemon-chicken Risotto

Creamy Spinach and Chicken Risotto

Chinese Chicken Risotto

Chicken and Ginger Risotto

Chicken and Zucchini Risotto

Thai Coconut Risotto

Chicken, Cardamom and Cashew Risotto

Duck and Blackberry Risotto

Duck and Orange Risotto

Duck, Pomegranate and Wild Rice Risotto

Turkey and Prosciutto Risotto

Christmas Risotto

chicken & corn risotto with croutons

THIS RECIPE IS MADE EXTRA-SPECIAL WITH GARLIC CROUTONS, WHICH ADD EXTRA CRUNCH AND FLAVOR.

5 cups (1.25 L) chicken stock

½ cup (125 mL) butter

1 Tbsp (15 mL) oil

4 boneless chicken thighs, skinned and halved

1 onion, finely chopped

4 cloves garlic, minced

2 cups (500 mL) arborio rice

Salt and freshly ground black pepper

Few drops hot pepper sauce

2 tomatoes, seeded and chopped

4 oz (125 g) baby corn, halved

2 thick slices white bread, crusts removed, cubed

1 Tbsp (15 mL) chopped fresh cilantro

2 Tbsp (25 mL) freshly grated Parmesan cheese

1 Pour the stock into a saucepan and bring to a boil. Reduce the heat to a gentle simmer.

2 Meanwhile, melt half of the butter in a large skillet with the oil and cook the chicken for 5 minutes over a gentle heat until browned. Add the onion and half of the garlic and cook, stirring, for 2 minutes until the onion has softened but not browned. Stir in the rice and cook, stirring, for 2 minutes until the rice is well-coated in butter.

3 Add a ladleful of stock and cook, stirring, until the liquid is absorbed. Continue to add small quantities of stock until half of it has been used and the rice is creamy. Season and add the hot pepper sauce and tomatoes.

4 Continue adding stock until the risotto is thick but not sticky, about 25 minutes. Meanwhile, cook the corn in boiling water for 5 minutes, drain, and add to the risotto. Melt the remaining butter in a skillet add the remaining garlic and cook the bread cubes for 2 to 3 minutes, turning until browned all over.

5 Just before serving, sprinkle the risotto with herbs, stir in the cheese, turn into a warm serving dish, and top with the croutons.

chicken & tarragon mushroom risotto

TARRAGON IS A CLASSIC FLAVORING FOR CHICKEN. IT IS ONE OF THE SUBTLEST OF HERBS AND FORMS PART OF THE *FINES HERBES* MIXTURE.

5 cups (1.25 L) chicken stock

¼ cup (50 mL) butter

1 Tbsp (15 mL) oil

4 boneless chicken breasts, skinned

1 onion, finely chopped

2 cloves garlic, minced

4 large open cap mushrooms, peeled and sliced

2 cups (500 mL) arborio rice

1 Tbsp (15 mL) Dijon mustard

Salt and freshly ground black pepper

2 Tbsp (25 mL) chopped fresh or 1 Tbsp (15 mL) dried tarragon

4 Tbsp (50 mL) light cream

½ cup (125 mL) freshly grated Parmesan cheese

1 Pour the stock into a saucepan and bring to a boil. Reduce the heat to a gentle simmer.

2 Meanwhile, melt the butter in a large skillet with the oil and cook the chicken for 5 minutes, turning until browned. Add the onion, garlic, and mushrooms and cook for 2 minutes until the onion has softened but not browned. Stir in the rice and cook gently, stirring, until the rice is well-coated in butter. Stir in the mustard.

3 Add a ladleful of stock to the rice and cook gently, stirring, until absorbed. Continue adding small quantities of stock to the rice until half of the stock is used and the rice is creamy. Season and add the tarragon.

4 Continue adding the stock until the risotto is thick but not sticky, about 25 minutes. Stir in the cream and cheese and serve in a warm bowl.

smoked chicken & mango risotto

SMOKED CHICKEN HAS A WONDERFUL FLAVOR THAT GOES WELL WITH EXOTIC FRUITS SUCH AS MANGO.

5 cups (1.25 L) chicken stock

¼ cup (50 mL) butter

1 onion, cut into eight

1 clove garlic, minced

2 cups (500 mL) arborio rice

Salt and freshly ground black pepper

12 oz (350 g) smoked chicken, shredded

Few sprigs thyme

1 cup (250 mL) button mushrooms, wiped and quartered

¼ cup (50 mL) blanched almonds

1 large ripe mango, peeled and diced

Fresh sprigs thyme, to garnish

1 Pour the stock into a saucepan and bring to a boil. Reduce the heat to a gentle simmer.

2 Meanwhile, melt the butter in a large skillet and gently cook the onion and garlic for 2 minutes, stirring, until the onion has softened but not browned. Stir in the rice and cook, stirring, for a further 2 minutes until the rice is well-coated in butter.

3 Add a ladleful of stock and cook gently, stirring, until the liquid has been absorbed. Continue adding small quantities of stock until half of the stock has been used and the rice is creamy. Season and add the chicken, thyme sprigs, mushrooms, and almonds.

4 Continue adding stock until the risotto becomes thick but not sticky, about 25 minutes. Gently stir in the mango pieces and fresh thyme. Serve in a warm bowl.

chicken asparagus risotto

TENDER ASPARAGUS IS PERFECT WITH DELICATELY FLAVORED CHICKEN. TRY TO USE YOUNG ASPARAGUS SPEARS AND AVOID ANY TOUGH, LARGE SPEARS.

3¾ cups (950 mL) chicken stock

1¼ cups (300 mL) dry white wine

¼ cup (50 mL) butter

12 oz (350 g) lean chicken meat, skinned and shredded

1 onion, finely chopped

2 cloves garlic, minced

2 cups (500 mL) arborio rice

Salt and freshly ground black pepper

Large pinch saffron

4 oz (125 g) small asparagus tips

¼ cup (50 mL) freshly grated Parmesan cheese

1 Pour the stock and wine into a saucepan and bring to a boil. Reduce the heat to a gentle simmer.

2 Meanwhile, melt the butter in a large skillet and gently cook the chicken for 2 to 3 minutes, stirring, until browned. Add the onion and garlic and cook for 2 minutes until the onion has softened but not browned. Stir in the rice and cook for a further 2 minutes until the rice is well-coated in butter.

3 Add a ladleful of stock to the rice and cook gently, stirring, until absorbed. Continue adding stock to the rice until half of the stock has been used and the rice is creamy. Season well and add the saffron.

4 Continue adding stock until the risotto is thick but not sticky, about 25 minutes. Meanwhile, cook the asparagus tips in boiling water for 5 minutes. Drain well and stir into the risotto with the cheese and serve.

OPPOSITE SMOKED CHICKEN AND MANGO RISOTTO

chicken & artichoke risotto

ARTICHOKES ARE A TYPE OF THISTLE, AND ARE QUITE AWKWARD TO EAT ALTHOUGH THE TASTE IS WORTH IT. FOR SIMPLICITY, USE EITHER PREPARED ARTICHOKE HEARTS IN FLAVORED OIL OR CANNED ARTICHOKES.

4 cups (1 L) chicken stock

⅔ cup (150 mL) dry white wine

¼ cup (50 mL) butter

1 Tbsp (15 mL) oil

4 boneless, skinned chicken breasts

1 onion, finely chopped

2 cloves garlic, minced

2 cups (500 mL) arborio rice

Salt and freshly ground black pepper

Juice of 1 lemon

1 stick celery, chopped

8 artichokes in oil, drained and halved

2 Tbsp (25 mL) pimentos in brine, drained and cut into strips

3 Tbsp (45 mL) chopped fresh mixed herbs

3 Tbsp (45 mL) freshly grated Parmesan cheese

1 Pour the stock and wine into a saucepan and bring to a boil. Reduce the heat to a gentle simmer

2 Meanwhile, melt the butter in a large skillet with the oil and cook the chicken gently for 5 minutes, turning until browned. Add the onion and garlic and cook for 2 minutes, stirring, until the onion has softened but not browned. Stir in the rice and cook, stirring, for 2 minutes until the rice is well-coated in butter.

3 Add a ladleful of stock and wine and cook gently, stirring, until all of the liquid is absorbed. Continue adding small quantities of stock mixture until half of the stock has been used and the rice is creamy. Season and add the lemon juice and celery.

4 Continue adding stock for a further 20 minutes. Stir in the artichokes and pimentos. Continue cooking for a further 5 minutes, adding stock until the risotto is thick but not sticky.

5 Just before serving, stir in the herbs and cheese and serve in a warm bowl.

risotto alla cacciatora

THIS RECIPE COMBINES THE FLAVORS OF FRESH LEMON, WINE, TOMATOES, MUSHROOMS, AND COGNAC TO GIVE A DELICIOUS RISOTTO, PERFECT WITH TENDER CHICKEN.

4 chicken breast fillets

½ lemon

3 cups (750 mL) chicken stock

⅔ cup (150 mL) dry white wine

¼ cup (50 mL) butter

1 Tbsp (15 mL) oil

1 onion, finely chopped

1 clove garlic, minced

2 cups (500 mL) arborio rice

Salt and freshly ground black pepper

14-fl oz (398-mL) can chopped tomatoes and their juice

2¼ cups (550 mL) button mushrooms, wiped and sliced

2 Tbsp (25 mL) cognac

2 Tbsp (25 mL) chopped fresh parsley

1 Rub the chicken with the lemon and reserve. Pour the stock and wine into a saucepan and bring to a boil. Reduce the heat to a simmer.

2 Meanwhile, melt the butter in a large skillet with the oil. Gently fry the chicken for 5 minutes, turning until browned. Add the onion and garlic and cook for 2 minutes until the onion has softened but not browned. Add the rice and cook, stirring, until the rice is well-coated in butter.

3 Add a ladleful of stock and wine and cook gently, stirring, until the liquid is absorbed. Continue adding stock until half of it has been used and the rice is creamy. Season and stir in the tomatoes and mushrooms.

4 Continue adding stock until the risotto is thick but not sticky, about 25 minutes. Stir in the cognac and parsley and serve in a warm bowl.

OPPOSITE RISOTTO ALLA CACCIATORA

chicken with caramelized apple & brandy risotto

COOKING THE APPLE SLICES IN BUTTER AND BROWN SUGAR GIVES THEM A CARAMEL FLAVOR THAT COMPLEMENTS THE SIMPLE TASTE OF THE RISOTTO. DO NOT OVERCOOK THE APPLES AS THEY WILL BREAK UP AND LOSE THEIR TEXTURE.

5 cups (1.25 L) chicken stock

⅓ cup (90 mL) butter

1 Tbsp (15 mL) oil

8 oz (225 g) lean skinless chicken, cut into chunks

1 onion, cut into eight

1 clove garlic, minced

2 cups (500 mL) arborio rice

Salt and freshly ground black pepper

1 Tbsp (15 mL) dark brown sugar

2 dessert apples, peeled, cored, and sliced

2 Tbsp (25 mL) cognac

2 Tbsp (25 mL) chopped fresh parsley

1 Pour the stock into a saucepan and bring to a boil. Reduce the heat to a simmer.

2 Meanwhile, melt ¼ cup (50 mL) of the butter with the oil in a large skillet and gently cook the chicken for 3 minutes, stirring, until browned. Add the onion and garlic and cook for 3 minutes, stirring. Stir in the rice and cook for a further 2 minutes, stirring, until the rice is well-coated in butter.

3 Add a ladleful of stock to the rice and cook, stirring, until absorbed. Continue adding small quantities of stock until half of the stock has been used and the rice is creamy. Season well.

4 Continue adding stock until the risotto is thick but not sticky, about 25 minutes. About 5 minutes before the rice is cooked, melt the remaining butter in a separate pan, add the brown sugar and cook the apples, stirring, until browned. Stir the cognac, apples and pan juices, and herbs into the risotto. Serve in a warm dish.

risotto coq au vin

ENSURE THAT THE CHICKEN IS THOROUGHLY COOKED BY TURNING DURING COOKING AND TESTING TO SEE IF THE JUICES RUN CLEAR FROM THE THICKEST PART OF THE CHICKEN PIECE. IF LARGE PIECES OF CHICKEN ARE TO BE USED, COOK SEPARATELY IN THE OVEN AND SERVE WITH THE RISOTTO.

4 cups (1 L) chicken stock

⅔ cup (150 mL) red wine

⅓ cup (90 mL) butter

1 Tbsp (15 mL) oil

12 oz (350 g) chicken pieces

4 slices rindless smoked back bacon, chopped

12 button onions

2 cloves garlic, minced

2 cups (500 mL) arborio rice

Bouquet garni (parsley, thyme, and bay leaf)

1 tsp (5 mL) red wine vinegar

1 tsp (5 mL) sugar

2 cups (500 mL) button mushrooms, wiped

4 slices white bread, crusts removed and cut into triangles

1 Pour the stock and wine into a saucepan and bring to a boil. Reduce the heat to a gentle simmer.

2 Meanwhile, melt ¼ cup (50 mL) of the butter in a large skillet with the oil and gently fry the chicken for 5 minutes, turning until browned. Add the bacon, onions, and half of the garlic and cook, stirring, for 2 minutes. Stir in the rice, and cook for a further 2 minutes, stirring, until the rice is well-coated in butter.

3 Add a ladleful of stock mixture to the rice and cook gently, stirring, until absorbed. Continue adding small quantities of stock to the rice until half of the stock has been used and the rice is creamy. Season well and add the bouquet garni, vinegar, sugar, and mushrooms.

4 Continue adding stock until the risotto is thick but not sticky, about 25 minutes. Meanwhile, melt the remaining butter with the rest of the garlic in a skillet and brown the bread triangles. Serve with the risotto.

lemon-chicken risotto

LEMON CHICKEN IS A FAVORITE CHINESE DISH. HERE IT TAKES ON A DIFFERENT TWIST, WITH A SLIGHT ORIENTAL FLAVOR AND A FRESH LEMON SAUCE.

4 cups (1 L) chicken stock

8 chicken legs

1/4 cup (50 mL) butter

1 Tbsp (15 mL) oil

2 leeks, trimmed and sliced

2 cloves garlic, minced

2 cups (500 mL) arborio rice

1 Tbsp (15 mL) light soy sauce

1 Tbsp (15 mL) cider vinegar

1 Tbsp (15 mL) light brown sugar

3 Tbsp (45 mL) dry sherry

1 Tbsp (15 mL) sesame oil

Juice of 1 lemon

Salt and freshly ground black pepper

1 Tbsp (15 mL) sesame seeds

Lemon slices, to garnish

1 Pour the stock into a saucepan and bring to a boil. Reduce the heat to a gentle simmer.

2 Meanwhile, cut two diagonal slits in each of the chicken legs. Melt the butter with the oil in a large skillet and gently cook the drumsticks for 5 minutes until browned. Add the leeks and garlic and cook for 2 minutes, stirring. Stir in the rice and cook for a further 2 minutes, stirring, until well-coated in butter.

3 Mix together the soy sauce, vinegar, sugar, sherry, sesame oil, and lemon juice and add to the pan. Add a ladleful of stock and cook, stirring, until absorbed. Continue adding small quantities of stock until half of the stock has been used and the rice is creamy. Season well and stir in the sesame seeds.

4 Continue adding stock until the risotto is thick but not sticky, about 25 minutes. Serve in a warm serving dish, garnished with lemon slices.

creamy spinach & chicken risotto

SPINACH REQUIRES VERY LITTLE COOKING. CHOOSE YOUNG SPINACH, RINSE, AND QUICKLY COOK IN THE WATER THAT REMAINS ON THE LEAVES. SPINACH IS PARTICULARLY GOOD SEASONED WITH NUTMEG.

4 cups (1 L) chicken stock

1/4 cup (50 mL) butter

1 Tbsp (15 mL) oil

12 oz (350 g) lean chicken, skinned and cut into chunks

1 onion, finely chopped

1 clove garlic, minced

3/4 cup (200 mL) quartered brown mushrooms

2 cups (500 mL) arborio rice

2/3 cup (150 mL) heavy cream

5 oz (150 g) spinach, trimmed and washed

4 Tbsp (50 mL) grated Parmesan cheese

1/2 tsp (2 mL) nutmeg

1 Pour the stock into a saucepan and bring to a boil. Reduce the heat to a gentle simmer.

2 Meanwhile, melt the butter in a large skillet with the oil and gently cook the chicken for 3 minutes turning until browned. Add the onion, garlic, and mushrooms and cook for 2 minutes until the onion has softened but not browned. Stir in the rice and cook gently, stirring, until the rice is well-coated in butter.

3 Add a ladleful of stock to the rice and cook gently until absorbed. Continue adding stock to the rice in small quantities until half of the stock has been used and the rice is creamy. Stir in the heavy cream.

4 Continue adding the stock until the risotto is thick but not sticky, about 25 minutes. Meanwhile, cook the spinach and drain well. Stir into the risotto with the cheese and nutmeg and serve.

chinese chicken risotto

THIS COLORFUL DISH, FLAVORED WITH CHINESE SPICES AND PACKED WITH VEGETABLES, IS A COMPLETE CHINESE MEAL IN ONE DISH.

5 cups (1.25 L) chicken stock

¼ cup (50 mL) butter

1 Tbsp (15 mL) oil

8 oz (225 g) lean boneless chicken, skinned and shredded

1 leek, sliced

2 cloves garlic, minced

1 tsp (5 mL) Chinese 5-spice powder

1 piece star anise, lightly crushed

1 Tbsp (15 mL) light soy sauce

2 cups (500 mL) arborio rice

1 carrot, julienned

1 red bell pepper, seeded and julienned

1 green bell pepper, seeded and julienned

7-oz (200-g) can water chestnuts, drained

¼ cup (50 mL) unsalted cashew nuts

¼ cup (50 mL) bean sprouts

1 Tbsp (15 mL) sesame oil

1 Pour the stock into a saucepan and bring to a boil. Reduce the heat to a gentle simmer.

2 Meanwhile, melt the butter in a large skillet with the oil and gently cook the chicken for 2 to 3 minutes, stirring until browned. Add the leek, garlic, 5-spice powder, star anise, and soy sauce. Cook for 2 minutes, stirring. Stir in the rice and cook for a further 2 minutes, stirring, until the rice is well-coated in butter.

3 Add a ladleful of stock and cook gently, stirring, until absorbed. Continue adding small quantities of rice until half of the stock has been used and the rice is creamy. Stir in the carrots, peppers, and water chestnuts.

4 Continue adding stock until the risotto is thick but not sticky, this should take about 25 minutes. Stir in the cashew nuts, bean sprouts, and sesame oil and serve in a warm dish.

chicken & ginger risotto

GINGER IS CONSIDERED TO BE ONE OF THE MOST IMPORTANT SPICES IN BOTH THE EAST AND WEST. FRESH GINGER IS ESSENTIAL IN MANY RECIPES AND IS VERY DIFFERENT IN FLAVOR TO GROUND GINGER, WHICH IS USED MAINLY IN BAKING.

5 cups (1.25 L) chicken stock

1/4 cup (50 mL) butter

1 Tbsp (15 mL) oil

12 oz (350 g) lean, skinned chicken, shredded

1 leek, trimmed and shredded

2 cloves garlic, minced

1/2-inch (1-cm) piece fresh ginger, chopped

2 cups (500 mL) arborio rice

Salt and freshly ground black pepper

Large pinch saffron

1 zucchini, shredded

8-oz (225-g) can bamboo shoots, drained

1 Pour the stock into a saucepan and bring to a boil. Reduce the heat to a gentle simmer.

2 Meanwhile, melt the butter in a large skillet with the oil and cook the chicken for 2 to 3 minutes, stirring, until browned. Add the leek, garlic, and ginger and cook for a further 2 minutes. Add the rice and cook for 2 minutes, stirring, until the rice is well-coated in butter.

3 Add a ladleful of stock and cook gently, stirring, until the liquid has been absorbed. Continue adding stock until half of it has been used and the rice is creamy. Season and add the saffron and zucchini.

4 Continue adding stock until the risotto is thick but not sticky, about 25 minutes. Stir in the bamboo shoots and spoon into a warm serving bowl.

chicken & zucchini risotto

CHICKEN LEGS ARE COOKED IN A RISOTTO THAT IS COLORED BY GRATED ZUCCHINI, WITH ADDED FLAVOR AND CRUNCH FROM PECANS. IT LOOKS AS APPEALING AS IT TASTES.

5 cups (1.25 L) chicken stock

1/4 cup (50 mL) butter

1 Tbsp (15 mL) oil

8 chicken legs

1 onion, finely chopped

2 cloves garlic, minced

2 cups (500 mL) arborio rice

Salt and freshly ground black pepper

3 zucchini, grated

1/2 cup (125 mL) shelled pecan halves

1/2 cup (125 mL) freshly grated Parmesan cheese

1 Pour the stock into a saucepan and bring to a boil. Reduce the heat to a gentle simmer.

2 Meanwhile, melt the butter in a large skillet with the oil and gently cook the chicken for 5 minutes, turning until browned. Add the onion and garlic and cook for 2 minutes, stirring, until the onion has softened but not browned. Stir in the rice and cook, stirring, for a further 2 minutes until the rice is well-coated in butter.

3 Add a ladleful of stock to the rice and cook, stirring, until absorbed. Continue adding small quantities of stock to the rice until half of the stock has been used and the rice is creamy. Season and stir in the zucchini and pecans.

4 Continue adding the stock until the risotto is thick but not sticky, about 25 minutes. Stir in the Parmesan cheese and serve in a warm bowl.

OPPOSITE CHICKEN AND ZUCCHINI RISOTTO

thai coconut risotto

THAI COOKERY USES COCONUT TO FLAVOR MANY DISHES. COUPLED WITH THE BLEND OF SPICES AND RED CHILES
IT MAKES A DELICIOUS MEAL.

3¾ cups (950 mL) chicken
stock

¼ cup (50 mL) butter

10 oz (300 g) boneless,
skinned chicken,
shredded

1 onion, finely chopped

2 cloves garlic, minced

1 tsp (5 mL) freshly
chopped lemongrass

1 tsp (5 mL) ground
coriander

1 tsp (5 mL) ground cumin

1 tsp (5 mL) turmeric

1 tsp (5 mL) chili powder

2 cups (500 mL) arborio
rice

2 red chiles, seeded and
sliced

1¼ cups (300 mL)
coconut milk

1 Tbsp (15 mL) chopped
fresh cilantro

1 Pour the stock into a saucepan and bring to a boil.
Reduce the heat to a gentle simmer.

2 Meanwhile, melt the butter in a large skillet and
cook the chicken gently for 2 to 3 minutes until
sealed. Add the onion, garlic, lemongrass, coriander,
cumin, turmeric, and chili powder and cook, stirring, for
2 minutes. Add the rice and cook, stirring, for a further
2 minutes until the rice is well-coated in butter.

3 Add a ladleful of stock and cook gently, stirring,
until the liquid has been absorbed. Continue
adding small quantities of stock until half of the stock is
used and the rice is creamy. Stir in the chiles.

4 Mix the coconut milk into the stock and continue
adding until the risotto is thick but not sticky,
about 25 minutes. Stir in the cilantro and serve in a
warmed bowl.

chicken, cardamom & cashew risotto

CARDAMOM IS NATIVE TO INDIA AND HAS A SPICY-SWEET FLAVOR AND A PUNGENT AROMA. EITHER THE WHOLE POD OR THE SEEDS CAN BE USED.

5 cups (1.25 L) chicken stock

¼ cup (50 mL) butter

1 Tbsp (15 mL) oil

12 oz (350 g) lean boneless chicken, skinned and shredded

1 onion, sliced

2 cloves garlic, minced

1 tsp (5 mL) ground cinnamon

6 cardamom pods or 3 tsp (25 mL) cardamom seeds

½ tsp (2 mL) chili powder

1 tsp (5 mL) fennel seeds

½ cup (125 mL) unsalted cashew nuts

2 cups (500 mL) arborio rice

Large pinch saffron

Salt and freshly ground black pepper

¼ cup (50 mL) golden raisins

1 Pour the stock into a saucepan and bring to a boil. Reduce the heat to a gentle simmer.

2 Meanwhile, melt the butter in a large skillet with the oil and gently fry the chicken for 5 minutes, stirring. Add the onion, garlic, cinnamon, cardamom pods or seeds, chili powder, fennel seeds, and cashew nuts. Cook for 2 minutes, stirring, until the onion has softened. Add the rice and cook for 2 minutes, stirring until the rice is well-coated in butter.

3 Add a ladleful of stock to the pan and cook, stirring, until absorbed. Continue adding small quantities of stock to the rice until half of the stock has been used and the rice is creamy. Sprinkle in the saffron and season. Stir in the golden raisins.

4 Continue adding the stock until the risotto is thick but not sticky, about 25 minutes. Serve in a warmed bowl.

duck & blackberry risotto

BLACKBERRIES ARE A REALLY JUICY, TASTY FRUIT AND ARE BEST USED FRESH. IF FRESH BERRIES ARE UNAVAILABLE, USE FROZEN OR CANNED.

4 cups (1 L) chicken stock

¼ cup (50 mL) butter

1 Tbsp (15 mL) oil

4 duck breast portions

1 onion, finely chopped

1 clove garlic, minced

2 cups (500 mL) arborio rice

Salt and freshly ground black pepper

⅔ cup (150 mL) dry vermouth

2 Tbsp (25 mL) chopped fresh thyme

¾ cup (200 mL) blackberries

1 Pour the stock into a saucepan and bring to a boil. Reduce the heat to a gentle simmer.

2 Meanwhile, melt the butter in a large skillet with the oil and gently cook the duck for 5 minutes, turning until browned. Add the onion and garlic and cook for 2 minutes until the onion is softened but not browned. Stir in the rice and cook for a further 2 minutes until the rice is coated in butter.

3 Add a ladleful of stock to the rice and cook gently, stirring, until absorbed. Continue adding stock to the rice until half of the stock has been used and the rice is creamy. Season well and add the vermouth and half of the thyme to the rice.

4 Continue adding stock until the risotto is thick but not sticky, about 25 minutes. Stir in the remaining thyme and blackberries and serve in a warmed dish.

duck & orange risotto

DUCK IS RICH FLAVORFUL MEAT BEAUTIFULLY COMPLEMENTED BY TANGY CITRUS FRUITS.

4 duck breasts

1 Tbsp (15 mL) soy sauce

2 Tbsp (25 mL) liquid honey

2 tsp (10 mL) ground ginger

3¾ cups (950 mL) chicken stock

1¼ cups (300 mL) orange juice

¼ cup (50 mL) butter

1 onion, finely chopped

1 clove garlic, minced

2 cups (500 mL) arborio rice

Salt and freshly ground black pepper

1 large orange, peeled and cut into segments

2 Tbsp (25 mL) chopped fresh parsley

1 Heat the oven to 400°F (200°C). Cut slits in the duck breasts with a knife and put on a rack over a roasting pan. Mix together the soy sauce, honey, and 1 tsp (5 mL) ginger and brush over the duck. Roast the duck for 25 to 30 minutes until done.

2 Meanwhile, pour the stock and orange juice into a saucepan and bring to a boil. Reduce the heat to a gentle simmer.

3 Melt the butter in a large skillet. Add the onion and garlic and cook, stirring, for 2 minutes until the onion is softened but not browned. Stir in the rice and cook, stirring, for 2 minutes until the rice is well-coated.

4 Add a ladleful of the stock and orange juice mixture and cook gently, stirring, until absorbed. Continue to add small quantities of stock to the rice until half of the stock mixture has been used and the rice is creamy. Season and add the remaining ginger.

5 Continue adding stock until the risotto is thick but not sticky, about 25 minutes. Stir in the orange segments and parsley and serve topped with the cooked duck breasts.

duck, pomegranate & wild rice risotto

THE POMEGRANATE GROWS IN CALIFORNIA, ASIA, AND
MEDITERRANEAN COUNTRIES. IT IS ONE OF THE MOST
ANCIENT FRUITS, WITH A WONDERFUL COLOR AND FLAVOR.

4 boneless duck breasts

1 Tbsp (15 mL) olive oil

2 cloves garlic, minced

2 Tbsp (25 mL) lime juice

1 Tbsp (15 mL) alfalfa
  honey

4 cups (1 L) chicken stock

²⁄₃ cup (150 mL) vermouth

¹⁄₃ cup (90 mL) wild rice

¹⁄₄ cup (50 mL) butter

1 onion, halved and sliced

2 cloves garlic, minced

2 cups (500 mL) arborio
  rice

2 large open mushrooms,
  peeled and sliced

Salt and freshly ground
  black pepper

Juice of 1 lime

2 pomegranates, halved

Lime zest, to garnish

1 Heat the oven to 400°F (200°C). Cut slits in one side of the duck breasts. Mix together the oil, garlic, lime juice, and honey and use to brush over the duck. Cook the duck in the oven for 25 to 30 minutes, until done.

2 Meanwhile, pour the stock and vermouth into a saucepan and bring to a boil. Reduce the heat to a simmer. Heat the wild rice in a saucepan of boiling water for 10 minutes, then drain and set aside.

3 Melt the butter in a large skillet and gently cook the onion and garlic for 2 minutes until the onion has softened but not browned. Add the arborio rice and cook, stirring, for 2 minutes until the rice is coated in butter.

4 Add the wild rice and mushrooms and a ladleful of stock. Cook, stirring, until the liquid has been absorbed. Continue adding stock until half of the stock has been used and the rice is creamy. Season and add the lime juice.

5 Continue adding stock until the risotto is thick but not sticky, about 25 minutes. Squeeze the pomegranates over a juicer then carefully remove some of the seeds from the membranes and stir into the risotto; serve in a warmed bowl garnished with pared lime zest.

turkey & prosciutto risotto

ALL THE FLAVORS OF ITALY ARE PACKED INTO THIS RECIPE, INCLUDING PROSCIUTTO, BLACK OLIVES, BASIL, AND ITALIAN CHEESE. TRY TO USE THE LEAN WHITE MEAT, AS THE RED MEAT OF TURKEY IS HIGHLY FLAVORED.

5 cups (1.25 L) chicken stock

1/4 cup (50 mL) butter

1 Tbsp (15 mL) oil

8 oz (225 g) lean turkey meat, shredded

1 onion, finely chopped

2 cloves garlic, minced

2 cups (500 mL) arborio rice

Freshly ground black pepper

1/2 cup (125 mL) prosciutto, shredded

1/2 cup (125 mL) pitted black olives, quartered

2 Tbsp (25 mL) chopped fresh basil

4 Tbsp (50 mL) freshly grated Romano cheese

1 Pour the stock into a saucepan and bring to a boil. Reduce the heat to a gentle simmer.

2 Melt the butter in a large skillet with the oil and gently cook the turkey, stirring, for 2 minutes until browned. Add the onion and garlic and cook for 2 minutes, stirring, until the onion has softened but not browned. Stir in the rice and cook gently for a further 2 minutes, stirring, until the rice is well-coated in butter.

3 Add a ladleful of stock to the rice and cook, stirring, until absorbed. Continue adding small quantities of stock until half of the stock has been used and the rice is creamy. Season with black pepper.

4 Continue adding stock until the risotto is thick but not sticky, about 25 minutes. Stir in the prosciutto, olives, and basil and sprinkle the cheese on top. Serve in a warm dish.

christmas risotto

A CHRISTMAS DINNER ALL-IN-ONE RECIPE OR PERFECT FOR USING LEFTOVERS. THESE TRADITIONALLY COMPLEMENTARY INGREDIENTS MAKE A DELICIOUS DISH.

5 cups (1.25 L) chicken stock

1/4 cup (50 mL) butter

1 Tbsp (15 mL) oil

8 oz (225 g) lean turkey meat, cut into strips

4 pork and herb sausages, cut into chunks

4 slices rindless smoked bacon, chopped

1 onion, finely chopped

2 cups (500 mL) arborio rice

Salt and freshly ground black pepper

4 Tbsp (50 mL) cranberry relish

2 Tbsp (25 mL) chopped fresh sage or parsley

1 Pour the stock into a saucepan and bring to a boil. Reduce the heat to a gentle simmer.

2 Meanwhile, melt the butter in a large skillet with the oil and gently cook the turkey, sausages, and bacon for 3 minutes, stirring until the turkey has browned. Add the onion and cook, stirring, for 2 minutes until softened but not browned. Stir in the rice and cook, stirring, for 2 minutes until the rice is well-coated in butter.

3 Add a ladleful of stock to the rice and cook gently, stirring, until absorbed. Continue adding stock to the rice until half of the stock has been used and the rice is creamy. Season well and add the cranberry relish.

4 Continue adding the stock until the risotto is thick but not sticky, about 25 minutes. Sprinkle on the herbs and serve in a warm bowl.

OPPOSITE **CHRISTMAS RISOTTO**

RISOTTO WITH GAME

Guinea Hen with Yellow Bell Pepper Risotto

Pheasant and Juniper Risotto

Sherried Squab and Peppercorn Risotto

Honeyed Quail with Lime Risotto

Creamy Quail Risotto

Venison Steaks with Lemon Risotto

Venison with Kumquat-walnut Risotto

Risotto with Venison and Mixed Peppercorns

Rabbit and Basil Risotto

Rabbit Risotto with Mustard and Prunes

guinea hen with yellow bell pepper risotto

THE SWEETNESS OF YELLOW BELL PEPPERS TAKES THE EDGE OFF THE RICHNESS OF THIS FLAVORFUL MAIN-COURSE RISOTTO. SERVE WITH A FRUIT JELLY SAUCE IF LIKED.

Four 4-oz (125-g) guinea hen
   breasts, skinned

Salt and freshly ground black pepper

¼ cup (50 mL) butter

1 Tbsp (15 mL) olive oil

1 Tbsp (15 mL) vegetable stock

5 cups (1.25 L) chicken stock

2 shallots, peeled and finely chopped

2 yellow bell peppers, seeded and
   sliced

2 cups (500 mL) arborio rice

⅔ cup (150 mL) dry white wine

3 Tbsp (45 mL) heavy cream

2 Tbsp (25 mL) lemon juice

Lemon zest, to garnish

1 Season the guinea hen breasts on both sides. Melt the butter with the oil in a skillet until sizzling. Lay the breasts in the pan and cook for 5 minutes. Turn over and cook for a further 5 minutes or until golden and done. Remove from the pan, reserving the cooking juices, and keep warm.

2 Pour the stocks into a saucepan and bring to a boil. Reduce the heat to a gentle simmer.

3 Meanwhile, transfer the reserved cooking juices to a large pan and heat. Gently fry the shallots and yellow bell peppers for 2 to 3 minutes until softened. Add the rice, and cook, stirring, for 2 minutes until well-coated in the vegetable mixture.

4 Add the wine and cook gently, stirring, until absorbed. Ladle in the stock gradually until all the liquid has been absorbed and the rice is thick, creamy, and tender. This will take about 25 minutes.

5 Stir in the cream and lemon juice and adjust the seasoning. Serve the risotto topped with the guinea hen breasts, garnished with lemon zest.

pheasant & juniper risotto

JUNIPER BERRIES ADD A PUNGENT, FRESH TASTE TO THIS DISH, COMPLEMENTING THE RICHNESS OF THE PHEASANT.

Four 4-oz (125-g) pheasant breasts

Salt and freshly ground black pepper

2 Tbsp (25 mL) butter

1 Tbsp (15 mL) olive oil

2 tsp (10 mL) dried juniper berries, crushed

2 Tbsp (25 mL) dry gin

5 cups (1.25 L) chicken stock

2 medium leeks, trimmed and thinly sliced

1 large carrot, peeled and coarsely grated

2 cups (500 mL) arborio rice

²⁄₃ cup (150 mL) dry white wine

Juice and pared zest of 1 lemon

2 Tbsp (25 mL) snipped fresh chives

1 Trim each pheasant breast to remove any excess sinew and skin. Leave a neat covering of skin on each. Season lightly on both sides. Melt the butter with the oil in a skillet and gently fry the pheasant breasts, skin-side down, with the juniper berries for 5 minutes. Turn over and cook for a further 6 to 7 minutes until done. Drain, reserving the pan juices, discard the skin, and flake the flesh. Place in a heatproof dish, spoon over the gin, and keep warm.

2 Pour the stock into a saucepan and bring to a boil. Reduce the heat to a gentle simmer.

3 Transfer the pheasant pan juices with the juniper berries to a large pan and gently fry the leeks and carrot for 2 to 3 minutes until just softened. Add the rice and cook, stirring, for 2 minutes until well mixed.

4 Add the wine, lemon juice, and zest, and cook gently, stirring, until absorbed. Ladle in the stock gradually until half the stock is used and the rice becomes creamy. Stir in the pheasant.

5 Continue adding the stock until the risotto becomes thick and the rice is tender. This will take about 25 minutes.

6 Stir in the chives and adjust the seasoning before serving. Serve the pheasant breasts over the risotto, garnished with a few juniper berries.

sherried squab & peppercorn risotto

IN THIS RECIPE, SQUAB BREAST MEAT IS SOAKED IN SHERRY AND ADDED TO A MUSHROOM RISOTTO
FLAVORED WITH THYME.

Two 10-oz (300-g) squabs, prepared

Salt and freshly ground black pepper

2 Tbsp (25 mL) butter

1 Tbsp (15 mL) vegetable oil

3 Tbsp (45 mL) medium sherry

5 cups (1.25 L) chicken stock

6 shallots, finely sliced

1 clove garlic, minced

2 large mushrooms, sliced

2 cups (500 mL) arborio rice

1 Tbsp (15 mL) chopped fresh or 1 tsp (5 mL) dried thyme

1 Tbsp (15 mL) pickled green peppercorns

Fresh thyme, to garnish

1 Slice off the legs and wings from the squabs. Separate and pull out the wishbone. Pull the skin away from the breasts and back. Cut down either side of the breast bone to split the birds in half. Wash and pat dry. Lightly season on both sides. Melt the butter with the oil and gently fry the squab portions for 10 to 12 minutes, turning occasionally, until done. Drain, reserving the pan juices, and flake the squab flesh from the bone. Place in a heatproof dish and spoon over the sherry. Cover and keep warm.

2 Pour the stock into a saucepan and bring to a boil. Reduce the heat to a gentle simmer.

3 Transfer the reserved squab juices to a large pan and gently fry the shallots, garlic, and mushrooms for 3 to 4 minutes until just softened. Add the rice and cook, stirring, for 2 minutes until well-mixed.

4 Add a ladleful of stock and cook gently, stirring, until absorbed. Continue ladling the stock into the rice until half the stock has been used and the rice becomes creamy. Stir in the thyme, peppercorns, and squab flesh.

5 Continue adding the stock until the risotto becomes thick and tender. This will take about 25 minutes and should not be hurried. Adjust the seasoning and serve garnished with thyme.

honeyed quail with lime risotto

THESE LITTLE BIRDS HAVE A RICH FLAVOR, ACCENTED IN
THIS RECIPE BY TANGY LIME AND ORIENTAL INGREDIENTS.

Four 6-oz (175-g) quails

2 Tbsp (25 mL) butter

1 Tbsp (15 mL) vegetable
oil

2 Tbsp (25 mL) liquid
honey

1 Tbsp (15 mL) dark soy
sauce

5 cups (1.25 L) chicken
stock

1 bunch scallions, trimmed
and shredded

1 clove garlic, finely
chopped

2 cups (500 mL) arborio
rice

Salt and freshly ground
black pepper

3 Tbsp (45 mL) dry sherry

Grated zest and juice of
1 lime

2 Tbsp (25 mL) chopped
fresh cilantro

Lime wedges and fresh
cilantro, to garnish

1 Preheat the oven to 450°F (230°C). Wash and pat
dry the quails. Melt the butter with the oil in a
skillet until sizzling, then fry the quails until browned on
all sides. Drain, reserving the pan juices, and place in a
roasting pan.

2 Mix 1 Tbsp (15 mL) honey with the soy sauce and
brush over the quails. Bake in the hot oven for
5 minutes, turn them over, baste, and bake for a further
6 to 7 minutes until cooked through. Drain, reserving the
pan juices, and keep warm.

3 Meanwhile, pour the stock into a saucepan and
bring to a boil. Reduce the heat to a gentle simmer.

4 Transfer the reserved skillet juices to a large pan
and gently fry the scallions and garlic for 2 to
3 minutes until softened. Add the rice and cook, stirring,
for 2 minutes until well-coated in the onion mixture.

5 Season and add the sherry, the reserved roasting
juices, and a ladleful of stock. Cook gently, stirring,
until absorbed. Continue ladling in the stock until all
the liquid is absorbed and the rice is thick, creamy, and
tender. Keep the heat moderate. This will take about
25 minutes.

6 Stir in the remaining honey, the lime juice and zest,
and the chopped cilantro. Adjust the seasoning if
necessary. Serve with the roasted quail, garnished with
lime zest and cilantro.

creamy quail risotto

A VERY RICH CREAMY MIXTURE OF ROASTED QUAIL WITH THE FLAVORS OF BACON, COGNAC, AND RAISINS.

Four 6-oz (175-g) quails, prepared

2 Tbsp (25 mL) butter

1 Tbsp (15 mL) olive oil

5 cups (1.25 L) chicken stock

1 medium red onion, finely chopped

1 Tbsp (15 mL) lemon juice

4 slices rindless bacon, chopped

2 cups (500 mL) arborio rice

Salt and freshly ground black pepper

1/3 cup (90 mL) seedless raisins

4 Tbsp (50 mL) cognac

2 Tbsp (25 mL) heavy cream

1 Preheat the oven to 450°F (230°C). Wash and pat dry the quails. Melt the butter with the oil in a skillet until sizzling, then fry the quails until browned on all sides. Drain, reserving the pan juices, and place in a roasting pan. Bake for 5 minutes, turn over, baste, then bake for a further 6 to 7 minutes until done. Drain, reserving any juices, and keep warm.

2 Meanwhile, pour the stock into a saucepan and bring to a boil. Reduce the heat to a gentle simmer.

3 Transfer the skillet juices to a large pan and heat. Fry the onion with the lemon juice and bacon for 4 to 5 minutes until golden. Lower the heat and add the rice. Cook, stirring, for 2 minutes until well-coated.

4 Season and add the raisins, cognac, cream, and a ladleful of stock and cook gently, stirring, until absorbed. Continue ladling the stock into the rice until all the liquid is absorbed and the rice becomes thick, creamy, and tender, about 25 minutes on moderate heat.

5 Peel off the skin from the quails and discard. Flake the cooked flesh from the bones and add to the risotto. Heat through for a further 2 to 3 minutes then serve on warmed plates.

venison steaks with lemon risotto

VENISON HAS A STRONG FLAVOR, AND IN THIS RECIPE IT IS COMPLEMENTED BY THE FRESHNESS OF LEMON AND THE DELICATE FRAGRANCE OF LEMONGRASS.

Four 5-oz (150-g) venison steaks

Salt and freshly ground black pepper

2 Tbsp (25 mL) butter

1 Tbsp (15 mL) olive oil

Finely grated zest and juice of 1 lemon

1 Tbsp (15 mL) clear honey

5 cups (1.25 L) vegetable stock

6 shallots, finely sliced

1 clove garlic, minced

2 cups (500 mL) arborio rice

1 stalk lemongrass, bruised

1 bunch scallions, trimmed and shredded

Lemon wedges, to serve

1 Season the steaks on both sides. Melt the butter with the oil in a skillet until sizzling, and add the steaks, lemon zest and juice, and honey. Cook the steaks for 5 to 6 minutes on each side until done and richly glazed in the honey-lemon mixture. Drain, reserving the pan juices, and keep the steaks warm.

2 Meanwhile, pour the stock into a saucepan and bring to a boil. Reduce the heat to a gentle simmer.

3 Transfer the pan juices to a large pan and reheat. Add the shallots and garlic and cook for 2 to 3 minutes until just softened. Add the rice and lemongrass and cook, stirring, for 2 minutes until well-mixed.

4 Add a ladleful of stock and cook gently, stirring, until absorbed. Continue ladling the stock into the rice until all the liquid is absorbed and the rice is thick, creamy, and tender. Keep the heat moderate. This will take about 25 minutes.

5 Discard the lemongrass. Stir in the scallions and adjust the seasoning. Serve with the venison steaks, accompanied by lemon wedges.

venison with kumquat-walnut risotto

KUMQUATS HAVE A SHARP, CITRUS TASTE, MAKING THEM IDEAL WITH RICH GAME LIKE VENISON. THIS IS A TRULY IMPRESSIVE RISOTTO.

Eight 3-oz (80-g) medallions of venison

Salt and freshly ground black pepper

2 Tbsp (25 mL) butter

1 Tbsp (15 mL) vegetable oil

4 oz (125 g) kumquats, sliced

1 Tbsp (15 mL) sugar

5 cups (1.25 L) beef stock

2 cups (500 mL) arborio rice

½ cup (125 mL) walnut pieces

1 Tbsp (15 mL) walnut oil

4 Tbsp (50 mL) snipped fresh chives

1 Season the medallions lightly on both sides. Melt the butter with the oil in a skillet until sizzling and fry the medallions over a moderate heat for 5 to 6 minutes on each side until done. Remove from the pan, reserving the juices, and keep warm.

2 Meanwhile, place the kumquats in a saucepan with ½ cup (125 mL) water and the sugar. Bring to a boil and simmer for 2 minutes. Set aside to cool in the liquid.

3 Pour the stock into a saucepan and bring to a boil. Reduce the heat to a gentle simmer.

4 Transfer the reserved juices to a large pan and reheat. Add the rice and cook, stirring, for 2 minutes until well-coated in the juices.

5 Add a ladleful of stock and cook gently, stirring, until absorbed. Continue ladling the stock into the rice until all the liquid has been absorbed and the rice becomes thick, creamy, and tender, about 25 minutes.

6 Stir in the kumquats and their cooking liquid until absorbed. Then add the walnut pieces, walnut oil, and snipped chives. Adjust the seasoning and serve with the cooked venison.

risotto with venison & mixed peppercorns

PUNGENT PEPPERCORNS AND SAVORY GAME MEATS, SUCH AS VENISON, ARE ALWAYS A DELICIOUS MATCH.

Four 5-oz (150-g) venison steaks

1 Tbsp (15 mL) mixed peppercorns, crushed

2 Tbsp (25 mL) butter

1 Tbsp (15 mL) olive oil

5 cups (1.25 L) beef stock

2 cups (500 mL) arborio rice

4 Tbsp (50 mL) cognac

1 Tbsp (15 mL) red currant jelly

1 tsp (5 mL) pickled pink peppercorns

1 tsp (5 mL) pickled green peppercorns

2 Tbsp (25 mL) chopped fresh parsley

Salt to taste

Flat leaf parsley, to garnish

1 Rub the venison steaks on both sides with the crushed peppercorns. Melt the butter with the oil in a skillet and fry the steaks for 10 to 12 minutes, turning occasionally, until done. Remove from the pan, reserving the juices, and keep warm.

2 Meanwhile, pour the stock into a saucepan and bring to a boil. Reduce the heat to a gentle simmer.

3 Transfer the reserved cooking juices to a large pan and reheat. Add the rice and cook, stirring, for 2 minutes until well-coated in the juices.

4 Add a ladleful of stock and cook gently, stirring, until absorbed. Continue ladling the stock into the rice until all the liquid has been absorbed and the rice is thick, creamy, and tender. Keep the heat moderate. This should take about 25 minutes.

5 Stir in the cognac, red currant jelly, peppercorns, and chopped parsley. Add salt to taste and serve with the venison steaks, garnished with parsley.

rabbit & basil risotto

THE TRULY ITALIAN FLAVORS IN THIS DISH – PEPPERY BASIL, RICH RED WINE, AND TANGY ORANGE – ARE THE PERFECT ACCOMPANIMENTS TO RABBIT.

1 lb (450 g) diced rabbit

Salt and freshly ground black pepper

2 Tbsp (25 mL) olive oil

5 cups (1.25 L) chicken stock

2 medium red onions, each cut into 8 portions

1 clove garlic, minced

2 cups (500 mL) arborio rice

$^2/_3$ cup (150 mL) red wine

1 Tbsp (15 mL) dark muscovado sugar

Finely grated zest and juice of 1 small orange

Small bunch fresh basil, shredded

1 Season the rabbit with salt and pepper. Heat the oil in a large saucepan until sizzling and fry the diced rabbit for 8 to 10 minutes until golden brown all over.

2 Meanwhile, pour the stock into a saucepan and bring to a boil. Reduce the heat to a gentle simmer.

3 Reduce the heat under the pan with the rabbit and add the onion and garlic. Gently fry for 2 to 3 minutes until softened. Add the rice and cook, stirring, for a further 2 minutes.

4 Add the red wine and sugar and cook gently, stirring, until absorbed. Ladle the stock into the rice gradually until it is all absorbed, and the rice is thick, creamy, and tender. This will take about 25 minutes.

5 Stir in the orange zest and juice. Adjust the seasoning and stir in the basil before serving.

rabbit risotto with mustard & prunes

THIS RISOTTO COMBINES RABBIT WITH RICH SHARP MUSTARD AND SWEET JUICY PRUNES.

$^3/_4$ cup (200 mL) dried prunes

1 lb (450 g) diced rabbit

Salt and freshly ground black pepper

2 Tbsp (25 mL) grain mustard

$^1/_4$ cup (50 mL) butter

1 Tbsp (15 mL) olive oil

5 cups (1.25 L) chicken stock

6 shallots, quartered

2 cups (500 mL) arborio rice

$^2/_3$ cup (150 mL) dry white wine

1 Tbsp (15 mL) chopped fresh or 1 tsp (5 mL) dried thyme

Fresh thyme, to garnish

1 Soak the prunes in water to cover, until plump, approximately 30 minutes. Meanwhile, season the rabbit and coat with the mustard. Melt the butter with the oil in a large saucepan until sizzling, then fry the rabbit for 8 to 10 minutes until golden all over.

2 Meanwhile, pour the stock into a saucepan and bring to a boil. Reduce the heat to a gentle simmer.

3 Reduce the heat under the pan with the rabbit and gently fry the shallots for 2 to 3 minutes until just softened. Add the rice and cook, stirring, for 2 minutes until well-coated in the rabbit juices.

4 Add the wine and thyme and cook gently, stirring, until absorbed. Ladle in the stock gradually until half has been used, then add the prunes. Continue ladling in the stock until it has all been absorbed and the rice is thick, creamy, and tender. This will take about 25 minutes.

5 Adjust the seasoning and serve garnished with fresh thyme.

OPPOSITE RABBIT RISOTTO WITH MUSTARD AND PRUNES

FISH RISOTTO

White Fish Wraps with Mustard Risotto

Curried Fish Risotto

Chili Monkfish Risotto

Sole and Fennel Risotto

Salmon and Caviar Risotto

Smoked Salmon and Dill Risotto

Trout and Shrimp Risotto

Mackerel and Orange Risotto

Smoked Trout with Peppercorn Risotto

Colcannon Risotto

Kipper and Apple Risotto

Tuna and Harissa Risotto

Anchovy, Pepper and Tomato Risotto

white fish wraps with mustard risotto

PLAICE AND SOLE ARE PERFECT FLATFISHES FOR FILLING AND WRAPPING. BAKED SEPARATELY IN THIS RECIPE,
THEY ARE FILLED WITH A SUN-DRIED TOMATO STUFFING AND SERVED ON A BED OF MUSTARD RISOTTO.

4 white plaice or other white fish fillets

FOR THE FILLING

½ cup (125 mL) whole-wheat bread crumbs

1 Tbsp (15 mL) chopped gherkins

1 Tbsp (15 mL) capers

2 scallions, finely chopped

2 Tbsp (25 mL) chopped sun-dried tomatoes

Salt and freshly ground black pepper

1 egg, beaten

4 Tbsp (50 mL) fish or vegetable stock

FOR THE RISOTTO

5 cups (1.25 L) fish or vegetable stock

¼ cup (50 mL) butter

1 onion, finely chopped

2 cloves garlic, minced

2 cups (500 mL) arborio rice

3 Tbsp (45 mL) Dijon mustard

Salt and freshly ground black pepper

2 Tbsp (25 mL) chopped fresh parsley

3 Tbsp (45 mL) freshly grated Romano cheese

1 Cut each fish fillet in half lengthwise. Combine all the stuffing ingredients except the stock, and spoon onto each fillet. Roll up the fish, starting at the wider end. Place in a shallow ovenproof dish and pour the stock around the wraps. Set aside.

2 Pour the stock for the risotto into a saucepan and bring to a boil. Reduce the heat to a gentle simmer. Preheat an oven to 400°F (200°C).

3 Melt the butter in a large skillet and gently cook the onion and garlic for 2 minutes, stirring, until the onion has softened but not browned. Stir in the rice and cook for a further 2 minutes, stirring, until the rice is well-coated. Put the fish in the hot oven and cook for 20 minutes at 400°F (200°C).

4 Meanwhile, add a ladleful of stock to the rice and cook gently, stirring, until absorbed. Continue adding small quantities of stock to the rice until half of the stock has been used. Stir in the mustard and season well.

5 Continue adding stock until the risotto is thick but not sticky, about 25 minutes. Stir in the parsley and cheese. Spoon the risotto into a warmed dish and top with the hot fish wraps.

curried fish risotto

FISH AND CURRY SPICES GO VERY WELL TOGETHER. THIS CURRY IS RELATIVELY MILD AND IS ENHANCED BY THE ADDITION OF GROUND ALMONDS FOR EXTRA FLAVOR.

5 cups (1.25 L) fish stock

¼ cup (50 mL) butter

1 onion, quartered

3 cloves garlic, minced

1 tsp (5 mL) ground cumin

1 tsp (5 mL) ground coriander

1 tsp (5 mL) garam masala

1 tsp (5 mL) chili powder

Large pinch turmeric

2 cups (500 mL) arborio rice

¼ cup (50 mL) ground almonds

Salt and freshly ground black pepper

3 Tbsp (45 mL) mango chutney

10 oz (300 g) cod fillets, cut into large chunks

⅔ cup (150 mL) heavy cream

2 Tbsp (25 mL) golden raisins

2 Tbsp (25 mL) toasted slivered almonds

2 Tbsp (25 mL) chopped fresh cilantro

1 Pour the stock into a saucepan and bring to a boil. Reduce the heat to a gentle simmer.

2 Meanwhile, melt the butter in a large skillet and gently cook the onion, garlic, cumin, coriander, garam masala, chili powder, and turmeric for 2 minutes, stirring, until the onion softens. Stir in the rice and gently cook for a further 2 minutes, stirring, until the rice is well-coated in butter.

3 Add a ladleful of stock and gently cook, stirring, until absorbed. Continue adding small quantities of stock until half has been used. Add the ground almonds, seasoning, and mango chutney.

4 Continue adding stock for a further 15 minutes. Stir in the fish and cream and cook for 10 minutes, adding stock until the risotto is thick but not sticky.

5 Just before serving, stir in the golden raisins, almonds, and cilantro. Serve in a warm dish.

chili monkfish risotto

CHILES AND LIMES ARE SYNONYMOUS WITH MEXICO, AND BOTH FEATURE IN THIS HOT RISOTTO DISH. FOR A MILDER RECIPE, REDUCE THE NUMBER OF CHILES AND REMOVE THE SEEDS BEFORE COOKING.

4 cups (1 L) fish stock

¼ cup (50 mL) butter

1 onion, finely chopped

2 cloves garlic, minced

1 tsp (5 mL) chili powder

2 cups (500 mL) arborio rice

Salt and freshly ground black pepper

7-fl oz (200-mL) can chopped tomatoes

2 green chiles, chopped

2 Tbsp (25 mL) tomato paste

Juice of 1 lime

12 oz (350 g) monkfish, skinned, boned, and cut into large chunks

2 Tbsp (25 mL) chopped fresh basil

2 Tbsp (25 mL) freshly grated Romano cheese

1 Pour the stock into a saucepan and bring to a boil. Reduce the heat to a gentle simmer.

2 Meanwhile, melt the butter in a large skillet and gently cook the onion, garlic, and chili powder, stirring, for 2 minutes until the onion has softened but not browned. Stir in the rice and cook gently, stirring, for a further 2 minutes until the rice is well-coated in butter.

3 Add a ladleful of stock to the rice and cook, stirring, until absorbed. Continue adding small quantities of stock until half has been used. Season well and add the tomatoes, chiles, tomato paste, and lime juice.

4 Continue adding stock for a further 15 minutes. Stir in the monkfish and continue cooking and adding stock for a further 10 minutes until the risotto is thick but not sticky.

5 Just before serving add the basil and cheese and serve in a warm dish.

sole & fennel risotto

SOLE IS A BEAUTIFULLY DELICATE FISH SUPERB WITH FENNEL'S ANISEED FLAVOR. IF THE FENNEL BULB IS INTACT,
USE THE FRONDS AS A GARNISH.

3¾ cups (950 mL) fish
stock

1¼ cups (300 mL) dry
white wine

¼ cup (50 mL) butter

1 red onion, halved and
sliced

1 clove garlic, minced

1¼ cups (300 mL) arborio
rice

¾ cup (200 mL) wild rice

1 Tbsp (15 mL) fennel
seeds

Juice and zest of 1 lime

1 bulb fennel, sliced

10 oz (300 g) sole fillets,
skinned and cut into
strips

2 Tbsp (25 mL) chopped
fresh dill

2 Tbsp (25 mL) freshly
grated Romano cheese

Lime zest, to garnish

1 Pour the stock and wine into a saucepan and bring
to a boil. Reduce the heat to a gentle simmer.

2 Meanwhile, melt the butter in a large skillet and
gently cook the onion and garlic, stirring, for
2 minutes until the onion has softened. Stir in the rices
and cook gently, stirring, for a further 2 minutes until the
rice is well-coated in butter.

3 Add a ladleful of stock mixture to the rice and cook
gently, stirring, until absorbed. Continue adding
stock mixture until half has been used. Stir in the fennel
seeds, lime juice and zest, and fennel slices.

4 Continue adding stock for 15 minutes. Stir in the
sole and cook for a further 10 minutes, adding stock
until the risotto is thick but not sticky.

5 Just before serving add the dill and cheese. Serve in
a warmed dish, garnished with lime zest.

salmon & caviar risotto

LUMPFISH CAVIAR IS USED AS A CAVIAR SUBSTITUTE IN THIS DISH. LUMPFISH ARE ABUNDANT IN COLD SEAS AND THEIR EGGS ARE COLLECTED AND DYED TO PRODUCE THIS INEXPENSIVE SUBSTITUTE FOR REAL CAVIAR.

5 cups (1.25 L) fish stock

¼ cup (50 mL) butter

1 onion, fine chopped

2 cloves garlic, minced

2 cups (500 mL) arborio rice

Freshly ground black pepper

12 oz (350 g) salmon fillet, skinned, boned, and cut into large cubes

2-oz (50-g) jar black lumpfish caviar

2 scallions, sliced

4 Tbsp (50 mL) sour cream

2 Tbsp (25 mL) freshly grated Parmesan cheese

1   Pour the stock into a saucepan and bring to a boil. Reduce the heat to a gentle simmer.

2   Meanwhile, melt the butter in a large skillet and gently cook the onion and garlic, stirring, until the onion has softened but not browned. Stir in the rice and cook gently, stirring, until all of the rice is well-coated in the butter.

3   Add a ladleful of stock to the rice and cook gently, stirring, until absorbed. Continue adding small quantities of stock for a further 20 minutes. Season with black pepper.

4   Add the salmon and cook, continuing to add the stock for a further 5 minutes until the risotto is thick but not sticky. Stir in the caviar, scallions, sour cream, and cheese and serve in a warm bowl.

smoked salmon & dill risotto

SMOKED SALMON IS ENHANCED BY THE ANISEED FLAVOR OF DILL.

3³/₄ cups (950 mL) fish stock

1¹/₄ cups (300 mL) dry white wine

¹/₄ cup (50 mL) butter

2 Tbsp (25 mL) lemon juice

1 red onion, cut into eight

2 cloves garlic, minced

2 cups (500 mL) arborio rice

Salt and freshly ground black pepper

1 tsp (5 mL) cayenne pepper

4 Tbsp (50 mL) chopped fresh dill

10 oz (300 g) smoked salmon, cut
  into strips

²/₃ cup (150 mL) light cream

Sprigs fresh dill, to garnish

1 Pour the stock and wine into a saucepan and bring to a boil. Reduce the heat to a gentle simmer.

2 Meanwhile, melt the butter in a large skillet and add the lemon juice. Gently fry the onion and garlic, stirring, until the onion has softened but not browned. Stir in the rice and cook gently, stirring, for 2 minutes until the rice is well-coated in butter.

3 Add a ladleful of the stock and wine mixture to the rice and cook gently, stirring, until absorbed. Continue adding the stock mixture until half of the stock has been used. Season well and add the cayenne pepper.

4 Continue adding stock for a further 20 minutes. Stir in the dill, salmon, cream, and continue cooking, adding stock for a further 5 minutes until the risotto is thick but not sticky. Serve in a warm bowl, garnished with dill.

trout & shrimp risotto

SMOKED TROUT HAS BEEN USED IN THIS FLAVORFUL AND COLORFUL DISH, BUT IF UNAVAILABLE, FRESH
TROUT FILLETS WOULD BE EQUALLY DELICIOUS.

4 cups (1 L) fish stock

⅔ cup (150 mL) dry white wine

¼ cup (50 mL) butter

1 leek, sliced

1 clove garlic, minced

1¼ cups (300 mL) arborio rice

¾ cup (200 mL) wild rice

1 green bell pepper, seeded and chopped

2 tsp (10 mL) fennel seeds, crushed

12 oz (350 g) smoked trout fillets, cut into chunks

4 oz (125 g) shelled cooked shrimp

1 Tbsp (15 mL) chopped fresh parsley

2 Tbsp (25 mL) freshly grated Parmesan cheese

Lime wedges, to serve

1 Pour the stock and wine into a saucepan and bring to a boil. Reduce the heat to a gentle simmer.

2 Meanwhile, melt the butter in a large skillet and gently cook the leek and garlic for 2 minutes, stirring. Add the rices and cook gently, stirring, for 2 minutes until the rice is well-coated in butter.

3 Add a ladleful of stock and wine mixture to the rice and cook gently, stirring, until absorbed. Continue adding small quantities of stock until half of the stock mixture has been used. Add the bell pepper and crushed fennel seeds.

4 Continue adding the stock for a further 20 minutes. Add the fish and shrimp and cook for a further 5 minutes, stirring gently, adding any remaining stock until the risotto is thick but not sticky. Check that the wild rice is tender; add more stock if necessary.

5 Add the parsley and cheese and serve in a warm bowl with lime wedges.

mackerel & orange risotto

ORANGE AND MACKEREL ARE A CLASSIC COMBINATION, THE OILY FISH BEING PERFECTLY OFFSET BY THE TANGY CITRUS FRUIT.

3¾ cups (950 mL) fish stock

1¼ cups (300 mL) orange juice

¼ cup (50 mL) butter

1 onion, finely chopped

2 cloves garlic, minced

2 cups (500 mL) arborio rice

Salt and freshly ground black pepper

2 tsp (10 mL) fennel seeds

1 stick celery, chopped

2 mackerel, cleaned, gutted, and halved lengthwise

1 Tbsp (15 mL) olive oil

2 oranges, peeled and cut into segments

1 Tbsp (15 mL) chopped fresh rosemary

1 Pour the stock and orange juice into a saucepan and bring to a boil. Reduce the heat to a gentle simmer.

2 Meanwhile, melt the butter in a large skillet and gently cook the onion and half of the garlic for 2 minutes, stirring until the onion has softened but not browned. Stir in the rice and cook gently, stirring, for a further 2 minutes until well-coated in butter.

3 Add a ladleful of stock and juice mixture and gently cook, stirring, until absorbed. Continue adding the stock and juice until half has been used. Season and add the fennel seeds and celery.

4 Continue adding the stock mixture until the rice is thick but not sticky, about 25 minutes. Meanwhile, brush the mackerel with the remaining garlic and oil and broil for 10 minutes, turning until cooked through. Remove as many bones as possible from the fish and cut the fish into large pieces. Gently stir into the rice with the orange sections and rosemary. Serve in a warm bowl.

smoked trout with peppercorn risotto

RED RICE AND MIXED PEPPERCORNS ADD COLOR AND FLAVOR TO THIS RISOTTO.

5 cups (1.25 L) fish stock

¼ cup (50 mL) butter

1 onion, finely chopped

2 cloves garlic, minced

1 tsp (5 mL) ground anise

3 Tbsp (45 mL) mixed peppercorns,
coarsely crushed

½ cup (125 mL) blanched almonds

1¼ cups (300 mL) arborio rice

¾ cup (200 mL) wild rice or red
Camargue rice

Salt

2 tsp (10 mL) almond extract

2 Tbsp (25 mL) chopped fresh
parsley

12 oz (350 g) smoked trout fillets,
cut into large chunks

2 Tbsp (25 mL) freshly grated
Parmesan cheese

1 Pour the stock into a saucepan and bring to a boil. Reduce the heat to a gentle simmer.

2 Meanwhile, melt the butter in a large skillet and gently cook the onion, garlic, anise, peppercorns, and almonds for 2 minutes, stirring, until the onion has softened but not browned. Stir in the rices and cook gently, stirring, for 2 minutes until the rices are well-coated in butter.

3 Add a ladleful of stock to the rice and cook gently, stirring, until absorbed. Continue adding small quantities of stock until half has been used. Season with salt and stir in the almond extract.

4 Continue adding stock until the risotto is thick but not sticky, about 20 minutes. Stir in the parsley, fish, and cheese and transfer to a warm serving dish.

colcannon risotto

THE TRADITIONAL RECIPE FOR COLCANNON COMES FROM IRELAND WHERE THE INGREDIENTS ARE POTATOES, CABBAGE, AND BUTTER. IN THIS VERSION, THE CABBAGE IS STIRRED INTO THE RICE, WHICH IS FLAVORED WITH FRESH HERBS AND CHEESE.

5 cups (1.25 L) fish stock

¼ cup (50 mL) butter

2 large onions, halved and sliced

1 clove garlic, minced

2 cups (500 mL) arborio rice

Salt and freshly ground black pepper

1 tsp (5 mL) freshly grated nutmeg

2 Tbsp (25 mL) chopped fresh parsley

12 oz (350 g) smoked cod, skinned and cut into large chunks

1½ cups (375 mL) shredded Savoy cabbage

¼ cup (50 mL) freshly grated Parmesan cheese

Freshly chopped parsley, to garnish

1 Pour the stock into a saucepan and bring to a boil. Reduce the heat to a gentle simmer.

2 Meanwhile, melt the butter in a large pan and gently cook the onion and garlic, stirring, for 2 minutes. Stir in the rice and cook gently, stirring, for a further 2 minutes until the rice is well-coated in butter. Add a ladleful of stock to the rice and gently cook, stirring, until absorbed. Continue adding stock until half has been used. Season well and add the nutmeg and parsley.

3 Continue adding stock for a further 15 minutes. Stir in the fish and cook for a further 10 minutes, adding stock until the risotto is thick but not sticky. Meanwhile, cook the cabbage in boiling water for 5 minutes. Drain well and stir into the risotto.

4 Just before serving, stir in the cheese and transfer to a warm serving dish. Garnish and serve.

kipper & apple risotto

KIPPERS ARE THE MOST COMMON SMOKED HERRING AND
ARE USUALLY SOLD WHOLE. LOOK FOR UNDYED KIPPERS
FOR THIS RECIPE.

3¾ cups (950 mL) fish
stock

1¼ cups (300 mL) apple
juice or cider

¼ cup (50 mL) butter

8 pearl onions, halved

1 clove garlic, minced

2 cups (500 mL) arborio
rice

Freshly ground black
pepper

Juice of 1 lemon

4 boned kippers, cut into
strips

1 Granny Smith apple,
sliced

3 Tbsp (45 mL) chopped
fresh sage

4 Tbsp (50 mL) light
cream

1 Pour the stock and apple juice or cider into a
saucepan and bring to a boil. Reduce the heat to a
gentle simmer.

2 Meanwhile, melt the butter in a large skillet and
gently cook the onions and garlic for 2 minutes.
Stir in the rice and cook gently, stirring, for a further
2 minutes until the rice is well-coated in butter.

3 Add a ladleful of stock mixture and cook gently,
stirring, until absorbed. Continue adding to the rice
until half has been used. Season with pepper and stir in
the lemon juice.

4 Continue adding stock for a further 20 minutes.
Stir in the fish, apple, sage, and cream and cook for
a further 5 minutes until the risotto is thick but not
sticky. Serve in a warm dish.

tuna & harissa risotto

HARISSA IS A ROBUST CHILI SAUCE, WHICH MAY BE MADE
AND STORED AT HOME, BUT IT IS MORE CONVENIENT TO
PURCHASE IT READY-MADE FROM MIDDLE-EASTERN
SPECIALTY STORES. ALTER THE QUANTITY OF HARISSA
TO YOUR LIKING.

5 cups (1.25 L) fish stock

¼ cup (50 mL) butter

1 onion, finely chopped

2 cloves garlic, minced

2 cups (500 mL) arborio
rice

Freshly ground black
pepper

1 Tbsp (15 mL) harissa
sauce

10 oz (300 g) fresh tuna,
cut into large pieces

1 oz (25 g) green beans,
trimmed

¼ cup (50 mL) pitted
green olives

2 Tbsp (25 mL) freshly
grated Parmesan cheese

1 Pour the stock into a saucepan and bring to a boil.
Reduce the heat to a gentle simmer.

2 Meanwhile, melt the butter in a large skillet and
gently cook the onion and garlic, stirring, for
2 minutes until the onion has softened but not browned.
Stir in the rice and cook for a further 2 minutes, stirring,
until the rice is well-coated in butter.

3 Add a ladleful of stock to the rice and cook gently,
stirring, until absorbed. Continue adding stock in
small quantities until half of the stock has been used.
Season with pepper and stir in the harissa sauce.

4 Continue adding stock for 15 minutes. Stir in the
fish and beans and continue to cook for a further
10 minutes, adding stock. Stir in the olives and cheese
and serve in a warm bowl.

anchovy, pepper & tomato risotto

ANCHOVIES APPEAR IN MANY ITALIAN RECIPES. THEY ARE VERY SALTY, SO DO NOT ADD ANY EXTRA SALT TO THE DISH AND CHOOSE GOOD-QUALITY FILLETS IN OLIVE OIL FOR BEST RESULTS.

5 cups (1.25 L) fish stock

¼ cup (50 mL) butter

1 onion, finely chopped

2 cloves garlic, minced

2 cups (500 mL) arborio rice

Freshly ground black pepper

1 red bell pepper, seeded and chopped

1 green bell pepper, seeded and chopped

2 green chiles, chopped

1 tsp (5 mL) chili sauce

4 oz (125 g) cherry tomatoes, halved

6 oz (175 g) anchovy fillets in oil, drained

2 Tbsp (25 mL) chopped fresh parsley

1 Pour the stock into a saucepan and bring to a boil. Reduce the heat to a gentle simmer.

2 Meanwhile, melt the butter in a large skillet and gently cook the onion and garlic, stirring, for 2 minutes until the onion has softened but not browned. Stir in the rice and cook gently, stirring, for a further 2 minutes until the rice is well-coated in butter.

3 Add a ladleful of stock and cook gently, stirring, until absorbed. Continue adding stock to the rice until half of the stock has been used. Season well with pepper and stir in the bell peppers, chiles, and chili sauce.

4 Continue adding stock until the risotto is thick but not sticky, about 20 minutes. Stir in the tomatoes, anchovies, and parsley, cook for a further 5 minutes and serve in a warm dish.

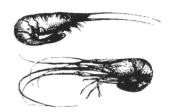

SEAFOOD RISOTTO

Sweet and Sour Shellfish Risotto

Ginger Scallop Risotto with Yellow Bean Paste

Scallop and Fennel Risotto

Red Pesto Risotto with Mussels on the Half-shell

Mussel and Shrimp Risotto

Risotto with Garlic Mussels

Mussels with Bacon-Saffron Risotto

Lobster Risotto

Prawn and Dill Risotto

Risotto with Flambéed Garlic Prawns

Shrimp Risotto with Sun-dried Tomatoes
and Porcini

Chili Shrimp Risotto

Oriental Crab Risotto

Mixed Seafood Saffron Risotto

Risotto Provençale

Risotto alle Vongole

sweet & sour shellfish risotto

FOR THIS ELEGANT RISOTTO, USE A MIXTURE OF COOKED SHELLFISH, SUCH AS SQUID, SHRIMP, CRAB, MUSSELS, AND LOBSTER.

5 cups (1.25 L) fish stock

3 Tbsp (45 mL) vegetable oil

4 shallots, finely chopped

2 cloves garlic, finely chopped

2 cups (500 mL) arborio rice

1 bunch scallions, trimmed and cut into 1-in (2.5-cm) lengths

4 oz (125 g) baby corn, sliced lengthwise

1 red bell pepper, seeded and thinly sliced

12 oz (350 g) cooked, mixed shellfish, thawed if frozen

2 Tbsp (25 mL) light soy sauce

1 Tbsp (25 mL) tomato paste

2 Tbsp (25 mL) red wine vinegar

2 tsp (10 mL) sugar

2 Tbsp (25 mL) chopped fresh cilantro

1 Pour the stock into a saucepan and bring to a boil. Reduce the heat to a gentle simmer.

2 Meanwhile, heat half the oil in a large pan and gently fry the shallots and garlic for 2 to 3 minutes until just softened, but not browned. Add the rice and cook, stirring, for 2 minutes until the rice is well-coated in the oil.

3 Add a ladleful of stock and cook gently, stirring, until all the stock is absorbed. Continue adding the stock until all the liquid is absorbed and the rice is thick, creamy, and tender. Keep the heat moderate. This will take about 25 minutes. Keep warm.

4 Heat the remaining oil in a wok or large skillet and over high heat stir-fry the scallions, baby corn, and red bell pepper for 1 minute. Add the shellfish and soy sauce and continue to cook for another minute. Blend together the tomato paste, vinegar, and sugar and add to the wok. Stir-fry for 1 minute until the vegetables are just tender.

5 To serve, carefully mix the stir-fried shellfish and vegetables into the risotto and serve sprinkled with chopped cilantro.

ginger scallop risotto with yellow bean paste

CHOOSE SMALL SCALLOPS FOR THIS RECIPE. THEY ARE SWEET AND JUICY AND REQUIRE VERY LITTLE COOKING, PERFECT FOR ORIENTAL DISHES.

5 cups (1.25 L) fish stock

2 Tbsp (25 mL) vegetable oil

1 bunch scallions, peeled and chopped

1 green chile, seeded and finely chopped

2 cups (500 mL) arborio rice

1 lb (450 g) fresh scallops, cleaned and trimmed

1-in (2.5-cm) piece fresh ginger, peeled and cut into thin strips

1 Tbsp (15 mL) light soy sauce

8 oz (225 g) snow peas, trimmed and thinly sliced

2 Tbsp (25 mL) yellow bean paste

1 tsp (5 mL) sugar

1 Pour the stock into a saucepan and bring to a boil. Reduce the heat to a gentle simmer.

2 Meanwhile, heat 1 Tbsp (15 mL) oil in a large pan and gently fry the scallions and chile for 1 to 2 minutes until just softened. Add the rice and cook, stirring, for 2 minutes until the rice is coated in the vegetable mixture.

3 Add a ladleful of stock and cook gently, stirring, until absorbed. Continue ladling the stock into the rice until all the liquid is absorbed and the rice is thick, creamy, and tender. Keep the heat moderate. This will take about 25 minutes. Keep warm.

4 Heat the remaining oil in a wok or large skillet and stir-fry the scallops and ginger for 1 minute. Add the remaining ingredients and stir-fry for a further 2 to 3 minutes until the scallops are done.

5 Carefully stir the scallop mixture into the rice and serve immediately.

scallop & fennel risotto

SCALLOPS FLAVORED WITH FENNEL AND CELERY GIVE THIS RISOTTO A DISTINCTLY SAVORY TASTE.

2 Tbsp (25 mL) olive oil

1 lb (450 g) scallops, halved or quartered if large

1 tsp (5 mL) celery seeds

5 cups (1.25 L) fish stock

2 Tbsp (25 mL) butter

2 medium leeks, finely chopped

2 sticks celery, trimmed and finely chopped

1 bulb fennel, trimmed, finely sliced, and fronds reserved

2 cups (500 mL) arborio rice

Celery salt and freshly ground black pepper

1/2 cup (125 mL) freshly grated Parmesan cheese

Chopped celery leaves, to garnish

1 Heat the olive oil in a large saucepan and gently fry the scallops and celery seeds for 3 to 4 minutes until done. Drain, reserving the pan juices, and keep warm.

2 Pour the stock into a saucepan and bring to a boil. Reduce the heat to a gentle simmer.

3 Melt the butter with the reserved pan juices in a large pan. Gently fry the leeks, celery, and fennel for 3 to 4 minutes until just softened. Add the rice and cook, stirring, for 2 minutes until well-mixed.

4 Add a ladleful of stock and cook gently, stirring, until absorbed. Continue ladling in the stock until all the liquid has been absorbed and the rice is thick, creamy, and tender. Keep the heat moderate. This will take about 25 minutes.

5 Mix in the scallops and season. Heat through for 2 minutes. Just before serving, stir in the Parmesan cheese. Serve garnished with chopped celery leaves and reserved fennel fronds.

red pesto risotto with mussels on the half-shell

LARGE MEATY NEW ZEALAND MUSSELS ARE RECOMMENDED, BUT ANY FRESH MUSSELS WILL BE DELICIOUS IN THIS RISOTTO. RED PESTO IS SIMPLY PESTO WITH THE ADDITION OF MINCED SUN-DRIED TOMATOES, IN AN AMOUNT YOU PREFER.

5 cups (1.25 L) fish stock

2 Tbsp (25 mL) butter

2 cloves garlic, finely sliced

1 medium red bell pepper, finely diced

2 cups (500 mL) arborio rice

⅔ cup (150 mL) red wine

3 Tbsp (45 mL) red pesto sauce

Salt and freshly ground black pepper

16 cooked New Zealand mussels on the half-shell

Basil leaves, to garnish

1 Pour the stock into a saucepan and bring to a boil. Reduce the heat to a gentle simmer.

2 Meanwhile, melt the butter and gently fry the garlic and red bell peppers for 2 to 3 minutes until just softened. Add the rice and cook, stirring, for 2 minutes until the rice is well-coated.

3 Add the red wine and cook gently, stirring, until absorbed. Gradually ladle in the stock until half has been used and the rice becomes creamy. Stir in the pesto, seasoning, and mussels.

4 Continue adding the stock until the risotto is thick and tender. Keep the heat moderate. This will take 25 minutes. Garnish and serve with crusty bread.

mussel & shrimp risotto

THIS SIMPLE RISOTTO USES COOKED MUSSELS AND SHRIMP, FLAVORED WITH DILL AND LEMON.

5 cups (1.25 L) fish stock

¼ cup (50 mL) butter

2 cloves garlic, minced

2 cups (500 mL) arborio rice

Finely grated zest and juice of 1 lemon

6 oz (175 g) shelled shrimp, thawed if frozen

6 oz (175 g) cooked and shelled mussels

2 Tbsp (25 mL) chopped fresh dill

1 Tbsp (15 mL) capers

Salt and freshly ground black pepper

Lemon wedges, to serve

1 Pour the stock into a saucepan and bring to a boil. Reduce the heat to a gentle simmer.

2 Meanwhile, melt the butter and gently fry the garlic and rice, stirring, for 2 minutes until the rice is well-coated in the butter.

3 Add a ladleful of the stock and cook gently, stirring, until absorbed. Continue ladling the stock into the rice until half the stock has been used and the rice becomes creamy. Stir in the lemon zest and juice, the shrimp, and mussels.

4 Continue adding the stock until the risotto becomes thick and tender. This will take about 25 minutes. Stir in the dill and capers. Season well and serve with lemon wedges.

121

risotto with garlic mussels

A TRADITIONAL COMBINATION OF MUSSELS IN THEIR SHELLS, WHITE WINE, GARLIC, AND CREAM, GARNISHED WITH CHOPPED PARSLEY.

3¾ cups (950 mL) fish stock

2 cups (500 mL) dry white wine

¼ cup (50 mL) butter

4 cloves garlic, minced

6 shallots, finely chopped

2 cups (500 mL) arborio rice

Salt and freshly ground black pepper

4 Tbsp (50 mL) chopped fresh parsley

3 lb (1.4 kg) fresh mussels in their shells, scrubbed

3 Tbsp (45 mL) heavy cream

1 Pour the stock and 1¼ cups (300 mL) wine into a saucepan and bring to a boil. Reduce the heat to a gentle simmer.

2 Meanwhile, melt 2 Tbsp (25 mL) butter in a large saucepan and gently fry half the garlic with the shallots for 2 to 3 minutes until softened but not browned. Add the rice and cook, stirring, for 2 minutes.

3 Add a ladleful of the stock and wine mixture and cook gently, stirring, until absorbed. Continue ladling the stock into the rice until half the stock has been used and the rice becomes creamy. Season well and stir in half the parsley.

4 Continue adding the stock until the risotto becomes thick and tender. This will take about 25 minutes. Keep warm.

5 Place the mussels in a large pan along with the cream, remaining butter and garlic, and wine. Cover with a tight-fitting lid and steam for 4 to 5 minutes over high heat, shaking the pan occasionally, until the mussels have opened. Discard any that fail to open.

6 Serve the mussels and the cooking liquid spooned over the risotto. Sprinkle with the remaining parsley.

mussels with bacon-saffron risotto

AN AROMATIC RISOTTO, PILED HIGH WITH TENDER FRESH MUSSELS, THAT IS PERFECT FOR AN INFORMAL SUPPER.

5 cups (1.25 L) fish stock

¼ cup (50 mL) butter

1 Tbsp (15 mL) olive oil

1 medium onion, finely chopped

4 slices lean bacon, finely chopped

2 cups (500 mL) arborio rice

Large pinch saffron

Salt and freshly ground black pepper

½ cup (125 mL) freshly grated
   Parmesan cheese

2 Tbsp (25 mL) chopped fresh
   parsley

3 lb (1.4 kg) fresh mussels in their
   shells, scrubbed

⅔ cup (150 mL) dry white wine

1 Pour the stock into a saucepan and bring to a boil. Reduce the heat to a gentle simmer.

2 Meanwhile, melt 2 Tbsp (25 mL) butter with the oil in a large pan and gently fry the onion and bacon for 2 to 3 minutes until just softened. Add the rice and cook gently, stirring, for 2 minutes until well-mixed.

3 Add a ladleful of stock and cook gently, stirring, until absorbed. Continue ladling the stock into the rice until half the stock has been used and the rice becomes creamy. Sprinkle in the saffron.

4 Continue adding the stock until the risotto becomes thick and tender. This will take about 25 minutes. Season and stir in the Parmesan cheese and half the parsley. Keep warm.

5 Place the mussels in a large saucepan with the remaining butter and the wine. Cover with a tight-fitting lid and steam over high heat for 4 to 5 minutes, shaking the pan occasionally, until the mussels have opened. Discard any that fail to open.

6 Serve the risotto with the mussels and cooking liquid spooned over. Sprinkle with remaining chopped parsley.

lobster risotto

TENDER LOBSTER IS MIXED WITH CREAM, CHEESE, HERBS, AND WINE – A LUXURIOUSLY RICH RISOTTO THAT MAKES AN EXCELLENT STARTER TO A LIGHT MEAL.

3¾ cups (950 mL) fish stock

1¼ (300 mL) cups dry white wine

2 Tbsp (25 mL) butter

1 Tbsp (15 mL) olive oil

6 shallots, shredded

1 clove garlic, minced

2 cups (500 mL) arborio rice

8 oz (225 g) cooked lobster meat, flaked

2 Tbsp (25 mL) chopped fresh parsley

2 Tbsp (25 mL) chopped fresh tarragon

2 Tbsp (25 mL) chopped fresh dill

4 Tbsp (50 mL) heavy cream

Salt and freshly ground black pepper

½ cup (125 mL) freshly grated Parmesan cheese

1 Pour the stock and wine into a saucepan and bring to a boil. Reduce the heat to a gentle simmer.

2 Meanwhile, melt the butter with the oil in a large pan and gently fry the shallots and garlic for 2 to 3 minutes until softened but not browned. Add the rice and cook, stirring, for 2 minutes, until well-coated in the shallot mixture.

3 Add a ladleful of stock and cook gently, stirring, until absorbed. Continue ladling in the stock until half is used and the rice becomes creamy. Mix in the lobster, half the herbs, and the cream.

4 Continue adding the stock until the risotto becomes thick, but not sticky. This will take about 25 minutes and should not be hurried.

5 Season. Just before serving, stir in the grated cheese and serve sprinkled with remaining herbs.

prawn & dill risotto

PRAWNS ARE VERY JUICY AND HAVE A SWEET TASTE – THEY REQUIRE VERY LITTLE COOKING. HERE THEY COMBINE WITH A WINE AND HERB RISOTTO TO MAKE A DELICIOUS DISH.

3¾ cups (950 mL) fish stock

1¼ cups (300 mL) plus 2 Tbsp (25 mL) dry white wine

¼ cup (50 mL) butter

4 shallots, finely chopped

2 cloves garlic, finely chopped

2 cups (500 mL) arborio rice

Salt and freshly ground black pepper

2 Tbsp (25 mL) chopped fresh dill

1 lb (450 g) raw shelled prawns

3 Tbsp (45 mL) heavy cream

1 tsp (5 mL) paprika

1 Pour the stock and 1¼ cups (300 mL) wine into a saucepan and bring to a boil. Reduce the heat to a gentle simmer.

2 Meanwhile, melt half the butter in a large pan and gently fry the shallots and garlic for 2 to 3 minutes until softened. Add the rice and cook, stirring, for 2 minutes.

3 Add a ladleful of the stock and wine mixture and cook gently, stirring, until absorbed. Continue ladling the stock into the rice until all the stock is used and the rice becomes thick, creamy, and tender. Keep the heat moderate. This will take about 25 minutes. Season well and stir in the dill. Keep warm.

4 Melt the remaining butter in a skillet and gently fry the prawns, stirring, for 2 to 3 minutes until pink all over. Stir in the cream and the remaining wine and cook for another minute.

5 Gently mix the prawns and creamy liquid into the rice and serve sprinkled with the paprika.

risotto with flambéed garlic prawns

LUXURIOUSLY BIG, JUICY PRAWNS AND SLIVERS OF GARLIC ARE FLAMBÉED WITH COGNAC AND STIRRED INTO A DELICATE TARRAGON RISOTTO.

5 cups (1.25 L) fish stock

¼ cup (50 mL) butter

1 medium leek, trimmed and finely chopped

1 bay leaf

2 cups (500 mL) arborio rice

Salt and freshly ground black pepper

2 Tbsp (25 mL) chopped fresh tarragon

Finely grated zest of 1 lemon

3 cloves garlic, finely sliced

16 raw prawns

3 Tbsp (45 mL) cognac

Fresh tarragon and lemon wedges, to garnish

1 Pour the stock into a saucepan and bring to a boil. Reduce the heat to a gentle simmer.

2 Meanwhile, melt half the butter in a large pan and gently fry the leek and bay leaf for 2 to 3 minutes until softened. Add the rice and cook, stirring, for 2 minutes until well-coated in the leek butter.

3 Add a ladleful of stock and cook gently, stirring, until absorbed. Continue ladling the stock into the rice until all the liquid has been absorbed and the rice is thick, creamy, and tender. Keep the heat moderate. This will take about 25 minutes. Discard the bay leaf, season well, and stir in the tarragon and lemon zest. Keep warm.

4 Melt the remaining butter in a skillet and gently fry the garlic and prawns for 2 to 3 minutes, stirring, until the prawns are pink all over. Warm the cognac, pour over the prawns and carefully ignite using a taper. Once the flames have died down, transfer the prawns to the risotto along with the juices. Gently mix in the juices and serve garnished with fresh tarragon and lemon wedges.

shrimp risotto with sun-dried tomatoes & porcini

DRIED VEGETABLES HAVE A MORE INTENSE FLAVOR THAN FRESH. FOR MAXIMUM SEASONING USE THE SOAKING LIQUID IN THE RISOTTO.

3¾ cups (950 mL) fish stock

2 cups (500 mL) sun-dried tomatoes, soaked as directed

1 cup (250 mL) dried porcini mushrooms, soaked as directed

3 Tbsp (45 mL) olive oil

2 medium red onions, finely sliced

2 cups (500 mL) arborio rice

⅔ cup (150 mL) extra-dry white vermouth

Salt and freshly ground black pepper

8 oz (225 g) cooked shelled shrimp, thawed if frozen

2 Tbsp (25 mL) chopped fresh parsley

1 Pour the stock into a saucepan and bring to a boil. Reduce the heat to a gentle simmer.

2 Meanwhile, drain the tomatoes and mushrooms, reserving the soaking liquid, and rinse well. Slice the tomatoes into thin strips, and cut up the mushrooms if large, or leave whole.

3 Heat the oil in a large saucepan and gently fry the onions, sun-dried tomatoes, and mushrooms for 5 minutes until just softened, but not browned. Add the rice and cook, stirring, until the rice is coated all over in the vegetable mixture.

4 Add the dry vermouth and ⅔ cup (150 mL) soaking liquid and cook gently, stirring, until absorbed. Gradually ladle in the stock until all the liquid has been absorbed and the rice becomes thick, creamy, and tender. Keep the heat moderate. This will take about 25 minutes.

5 Season and stir in the shrimp. Heat through for 2 minutes. Serve sprinkled with chopped parsley.

chili shrimp risotto

THIS RISOTTO HAS THE FLAVOR OF THAILAND WITH INGREDIENTS SUCH AS CHILES, COCONUT, SCALLIONS, LEMONGRASS, AND PEANUTS. IT IS AN IDEAL DISH TO SERVE ON A SPECIAL OCCASION.

3¾ cups (950 mL) fish stock

1 Tbsp (15 mL) vegetable oil

1 bunch scallions, trimmed and chopped

1 clove garlic, minced

1 red chile, seeded and finely chopped

2 cups (500 mL) arborio rice

1 stalk lemongrass, bruised

1¼ cups (300 mL) coconut milk

1 Tbsp (15 mL) Thai fish sauce

8 oz (225 g) shelled large shrimp, thawed if frozen

¼ cup (50 mL) crushed roasted peanuts

Shredded scallions and red chile, to garnish

1 Pour the stock into a saucepan and bring to a boil. Reduce the heat to a gentle simmer.

2 Meanwhile, heat the oil in a large saucepan and gently fry the scallions, garlic, and red chile for 1 to 2 minutes, until just softened. Add the rice and cook, stirring, for 2 minutes until well-coated in the scallion mixture.

3 Add the lemongrass, coconut milk, and fish sauce and cook gently, stirring, until absorbed. Gradually ladle in the stock until all the liquid has been absorbed and the rice is thick, creamy, and tender. Keep the heat moderate. This will take about 25 minutes.

4 Discard the lemongrass. Stir in the shrimp and cook for a further 2 minutes.

5 Serve sprinkled with chopped peanuts, and garnish with scallions and red chile.

OPPOSITE CHILI SHRIMP RISOTTO

oriental crab risotto

CHOOSE CRAB CLAWS THAT CONTAIN A LOT OF MEAT. IF SMALLER ONES ARE AVAILABLE, THEN USE 12 TO 16 FOR THIS RECIPE.

5 cups (1.25 L) fish stock

3 Tbsp (45 mL) vegetable oil

1 bunch scallions, trimmed and finely chopped

1 red bell pepper, seeded and sliced

1 clove garlic, finely chopped

½-in (1-cm) piece fresh ginger, finely chopped

2 cups (500 mL) arborio rice

8 large crab claws, cracked

1 tsp (5 mL) Chinese 5-spice powder

2 Tbsp (25 mL) dark soy sauce

2 cups (500 mL) finely shredded bok choy

2 tsp (10 mL) sesame oil

2 Tbsp (25 mL) snipped fresh chives

1 Pour the stock into a saucepan and bring to a boil. Reduce the heat to a gentle simmer.

2 Meanwhile, heat the vegetable oil in a large pan and gently fry the scallions, red bell pepper, garlic, and ginger for 3 to 4 minutes until softened. Add the rice and cook, stirring, for 2 minutes until well-mixed.

3 Add a ladleful of stock and cook gently, stirring, until absorbed. Continue to ladle in the stock until all the liquid is absorbed and the rice becomes thick, creamy, and tender. Keep the heat moderate. This will take about 25 minutes. Keep warm.

4 Heat the remaining oil in a wok or large skillet and stir-fry the crab claws with the 5-spice powder for 1 minute. Add the soy sauce and bok choy and stir-fry for a further 2 to 3 minutes until the leaves are tender and wilted. Mix in the sesame oil.

5 Spoon the stir-fried crab mixture over the rice and serve sprinkled with snipped chives.

mixed seafood saffron risotto

A SELECTION OF MUSSELS, CLAMS, SHRIMP, AND SCALLOPS ARE COOKED IN A WINE AND CREAM SAUCE AND SERVED WITH A FRAGRANT, GOLDEN RISOTTO.

5 cups (1.25 L) fish stock

¹⁄₃ cup (90 mL) butter

1 medium onion, finely chopped

2 cloves garlic, minced

2 cups (500 mL) arborio rice

Large pinch saffron

Salt and freshly ground black pepper

²⁄₃ cup (150 mL) dry white wine

4 Tbsp (50 mL) heavy cream

1 lb (450 g) fresh mussels in their shells, scrubbed

1 lb (450 g) fresh clams in their shells, scrubbed and soaked

8 oz (225 g) fresh scallops, cleaned and trimmed

8 oz (225 g) large raw shrimp in their shells

2 Tbsp (25 mL) chopped fresh parsley

1 Pour the stock into a saucepan and bring to a boil. Reduce the heat to a gentle simmer.

2 Meanwhile, melt ¼ cup (50 mL) butter in a large saucepan and gently fry the onion and half the garlic for 2 to 3 minutes until softened but not browned. Stir in the rice and cook, stirring, for 2 minutes until the rice is well-coated in butter.

3 Add a ladleful of stock and cook gently, stirring, until absorbed. Continue ladling the stock into the rice until half the stock has been used and the rice becomes creamy. Sprinkle in the saffron and seasoning.

4 Continue adding the stock until the risotto becomes thick, but not sticky. This will take about 25 minutes and should not be hurried. Keep warm.

5 Pour the wine into a saucepan and add the cream and remaining garlic and butter. Add the shellfish, cover with a tight-fitting lid and cook over high heat for 5 to 6 minutes, shaking the pan occasionally, until the mussels and clams have opened and the shrimp are pink. Discard any mussels or clams that fail to open.

6 Serve the risotto with the shellfish and juices spooned over, and sprinkle with the parsley.

131

risotto provençale

PACKED FULL OF THE SUNNY FLAVORS OF THE
MEDITERRANEAN, THIS DELICIOUS RISOTTO MAKES A
SUBSTANTIAL MAIN COURSE SERVED WITH CRUSTY BREAD
AND A CRISP SALAD.

- 3¾ cups (950 mL) fish stock
- 4 Tbsp (50 mL) olive oil
- 6 shallots, finely chopped
- 1 clove garlic, thinly sliced
- 1 yellow bell pepper, seeded and diced
- 2 medium zucchini, trimmed and diced
- 1 medium eggplant, trimmed and diced
- 2 cups (500 mL) arborio rice
- 1 tsp (5 mL) dried or 2 Tbsp (25 mL) fresh mixed herbs
- ⅔ cup (150 mL) dry red wine
- 14-fl oz (398-mL) can chopped tomatoes
- 1 tsp (5 mL) sugar
- Salt and freshly ground black pepper
- 8 oz (225 g) prepared baby squid, sliced into rings
- Few pitted black olives
- Fresh herbs, to garnish

1 Pour the stock into a saucepan and bring to a boil. Reduce the heat to a gentle simmer.

2 Meanwhile, heat the oil in a large pan and gently fry the shallots, garlic, bell pepper, zucchini, and eggplant for 4 to 5 minutes until softened. Add the rice and cook, stirring, for 2 minutes until well-mixed.

3 Add the herbs, wine, tomatoes, and sugar and cook gently, stirring, until absorbed. Gradually ladle in the stock until half has been used and the rice becomes creamy. Season well and stir in the squid.

4 Continue adding the stock until the risotto becomes thick and tender, about 25 minutes. Sprinkle with olives and fresh herbs and serve.

risotto alle vongole

IN ITALY, VERY SMALL CLAMS (VONGOLE) ARE USUALLY
SERVED WITH FETTUCINE, BUT THEY ADAPT VERY WELL TO
THIS RISOTTO DISH.

- 5 cups (1.25 L) fish stock or a mix of clam juice and fish stock
- 2 Tbsp (25 mL) olive oil
- 3 cloves garlic, sliced
- 3 small dried chiles, chopped
- 2 cups (500 mL) arborio rice
- Salt and freshly ground black pepper
- 3 lb (1.4 kg) clams, scrubbed and soaked
- ⅔ cup (150 mL) dry white wine
- 2 Tbsp (25 mL) chopped fresh parsley

1 Pour the stock into a saucepan and bring to a boil. Reduce the heat to a gentle simmer.

2 Meanwhile, heat the oil in a large pan and gently fry two-thirds of the garlic and half the chiles for 1 to 2 minutes until just softened but not browned. Add the rice and cook, stirring, for 2 minutes until the rice is well-coated in the oil.

3 Add a ladleful of stock and cook gently, stirring, until absorbed. Continue ladling in the stock until all the liquid has been absorbed and the rice becomes thick, creamy, and tender. Keep the heat moderate. This will take about 25 minutes. Season well and keep warm.

4 Place the clams in a large saucepan and pour over the wine. Add the remaining garlic and chiles. Cover with a tight-fitting lid, and cook over a high heat until they open, shaking the pan constantly. Discard any clams that fail to open.

5 To serve the risotto, spoon the clams with their cooking juices over each portion of rice and sprinkle with parsley.

OPPOSITE **RISOTTO ALLE VONGOLE**

SWEET RISOTTO

Chocolate and Vanilla Risotto

Chocolate Orange Risotto

Tiramisu Risotto

Cream Cheese and Apricot Risotto

Raspberry, Peach and Hazelnut Risotto

Summer Fruits Risotto

Lemon and Sultana Risotto

Sunshine Fruit Risotto

Apple, Pear and Cinnamon Risotto

chocolate & vanilla risotto

THIS IS A RICH INDULGENT DESSERT THAT IS NOT FOR THOSE COUNTING CALORIES.

4 cups (1 L) milk

¼ cup (50 mL) butter

2 cups (500 mL) arborio rice

2 Tbsp (25 mL) sugar

1 vanilla bean

3 oz (80 g) semisweet chocolate, grated

⅔ cup (150 mL) heavy cream

1 Heat the milk to a boil, then reduce the heat to a gentle simmer.

2 Meanwhile, melt the butter in a large skillet and gently cook the rice for 2 minutes, stirring, until the rice is well-coated in butter.

3 Add a ladleful of milk and cook gently, stirring until absorbed. Stir in the sugar and vanilla bean. Continue adding small quantities of milk for 20 minutes, stirring, until the milk has been used. Remove the vanilla bean from the rice.

4 Add the chocolate and cream and cook for a further 5 minutes. Serve in a warm dish.

chocolate orange risotto

CHOCOLATE AND ORANGE ARE AN IRRESISTIBLE COMBINATION. FOR A SPECIAL TOUCH, GRATE THE WHITE CHOCOLATE OVER THE RISOTTO JUST BEFORE SERVING, TO PREVENT IT MELTING TOTALLY.

4 cups (1 L) milk

¼ cup (50 mL) butter

2 cups (500 mL) arborio rice

4 Tbsp (50 mL) orange liqueur

⅔ cup (150 mL) orange juice

2 oz (50 g) milk chocolate, grated

2 oranges, peeled and cut into segments

1 oz (25 g) white chocolate, coarsely grated to garnish

1 Pour the milk into a saucepan and bring to a boil. Reduce the heat to a gentle simmer.

2 Meanwhile, melt the butter in a pan and gently cook the rice for 2 minutes, stirring, until the rice is well-coated in butter. Stir in the orange liqueur and orange juice and cook gently, stirring, until absorbed.

3 Add a ladleful of milk to the rice and cook, stirring, until absorbed. Continue adding small quantities of milk for a further 20 minutes. Stir in the milk chocolate and orange sections. Continue to cook for a further 5 minutes until the risotto is thick but not sticky. Sprinkle the white chocolate over the top and serve.

tiramisu risotto

THIS IS A TRADITIONAL, RICH DESSERT ASSOCIATED WITH, AND LOVED BY, ITALIANS.

3¾ cups (950 mL) milk

1¼ cups (300 mL) heavy cream

¼ cup (50 mL) butter

2 cups (500 mL) arborio rice

4 Tbsp (50 mL) strong black coffee

1 Tbsp (15 mL) cocoa powder

2 Tbsp (25 mL) sugar

3 Tbsp (45 mL) cognac

2 oz (50 g) coarsely grated semisweet chocolate

1 Pour the milk and cream into a saucepan and bring to a boil. Reduce the heat to a gentle simmer.

2 Meanwhile, melt the butter in a large skillet and stir in the rice. Cook gently, stirring, for 2 minutes until the rice is well-coated in butter. Mix the coffee, cocoa, sugar, and cognac together and stir into the rice with a ladleful of milk and cream mixture.

3 Cook gently, stirring, until absorbed. Continue adding the cream and milk in small quantities for a further 25 minutes. Stir in the chocolate and serve in a warm dish.

cream cheese & apricot risotto

CHEESE AND APRICOTS TASTE GOOD TOGETHER WHEN LIGHTLY SWEETENED. USE FULL-FAT CREAM CHEESE IF POSSIBLE AND RIPE APRICOTS FOR BETTER FLAVOR.

5 cups (1.25 L) apricot juice

¼ cup (50 mL) butter

2 tsp (10 mL) allspice

2 cups (500 mL) arborio rice

1 cup (250 mL) cream cheese

2 Tbsp (25 mL) confectioners' sugar, sifted

12 oz (350 g) fresh apricots, pitted and quartered

Lemon balm, to garnish

1 Pour the apricot juice into a saucepan and bring to a boil. Reduce the heat to a gentle simmer.

2 Meanwhile, melt the butter in a large skillet and gently cook the allspice and rice for 2 minutes, stirring, until the rice is well-coated in butter.

3 Add a ladleful of apricot juice and cook gently, stirring, until absorbed. Continue adding small quantities of juice to the rice until half has been used. Stir in the cream cheese and sugar.

4 Continue adding the juice until the risotto is thick but not sticky, about 25 minutes. Stir in the apricots and cook for a further 5 minutes. Serve garnished with lemon balm.

OPPOSITE TIRAMISU RISOTTO

raspberry, peach & hazelnut risotto

THIS COLORFUL COMBINATION OF INGREDIENTS IS USUALLY FOUND IN THE CLASSIC DESSERT PEACH MELBA. HERE, STIRRED INTO RICE SWEETENED WITH PEACH NECTAR, THEY ARE SENSATIONAL.

2½ cups (625 mL) milk

1¼ cups (300 mL) heavy cream

1¼ cups (300 mL) peach nectar

¼ cup (50 mL) butter

½ cup (125 mL) coarsely chopped hazelnuts

2 cups (500 mL) arborio rice

2 Tbsp (25 mL) confectioners' sugar

8 oz (225 g) canned or fresh peach quarters

⅔ cup (150 mL) raspberries

Sprigs mint, to decorate

1 Pour the milk and cream into a saucepan with the peach nectar and bring to a boil. Reduce the heat to a gentle simmer.

2 Meanwhile, melt the butter in a large skillet and gently cook the nuts for 1 minute, stirring. Add the rice and cook, stirring, for a further 2 minutes until the rice is well-coated in butter.

3 Add a ladleful of the milk, cream, and nectar mixture and cook gently, stirring, until absorbed. Stir in the sugar and continue adding the liquid in small quantities for a further 20 minutes.

4 Gently stir in the peaches and raspberries, cook for 4 to 5 minutes until the risotto is thick but not sticky. Serve in a warm dish, decorated with mint.

summer fruits risotto

NOTHING QUITE BEATS THE FLAVORS OF MIXED SUMMER FRUITS. STIR THEM VERY GENTLY INTO THE RISOTTO SO THAT THEY DO NOT BREAK UP.

3¾ cups (950 mL) milk

1¼ cups (300 mL) heavy cream

¼ cup (50 mL) butter

2 cups (500 mL) arborio rice

1 tsp (5 mL) ground cinnamon

2 Tbsp (25 mL) sugar

2 Tbsp (25 mL) kirsch

4 cups (1 L) mixed summer fruits such as strawberries, raspberries, blueberries, red and black currants

1 Tbsp (15 mL) chopped fresh mint

1 Pour the milk and cream into a saucepan and bring to a boil. Immediately reduce the heat to a gentle simmer, and keep simmering.

2 Meanwhile, melt the butter in a large skillet and gently cook the rice in it, stirring, until well-coated in the butter.

3 Add a ladleful of the milk and cream mixture and cook gently, stirring, until absorbed. Add the cinnamon, sugar, and kirsch and continue adding small quantities of milk and cream until the risotto is thick but not sticky. Gently stir in the fruit and mint and serve.

OPPOSITE SUMMER FRUITS RISOTTO

lemon & sultana risotto

THIS IS A TANGY DESSERT WITH FRESH LEMON JUICE AND ZEST, FLAVORED WITH NUTMEG.

3³/₄ cups (950 mL) milk

1¹/₄ cups (300 mL) heavy cream

¹/₃ cup (90 mL) butter

2 cups (500 mL) arborio rice

Juice and zest of 1 lemon

1 tsp (5 mL) nutmeg

2 Tbsp (25 mL) light brown sugar

¹/₂ cup (125 mL) sultanas

1 lemon, halved and sliced

1 Pour the milk and cream into a saucepan and bring to a boil. Reduce the heat to a gentle simmer.

2 Meanwhile, melt ¹/₄ cup (50 mL) of the butter in a large skillet and cook the rice for 2 minutes, stirring, until the rice is well-coated in butter.

3 Add a ladleful of the milk and cream mixture with the lemon juice and zest and cook gently, stirring, until the liquid is absorbed. Stir in the nutmeg and sugar, and continue adding small quantities of milk and cream for a further 20 minutes.

4 Stir in the sultanas and continue cooking for a further 5 minutes until the risotto is thick but not sticky. Meanwhile, melt the remaining butter in a separate skillet and cook the lemon slices for 2 to 3 minutes, turning. Stir the contents of the pan into the risotto and serve in a warm dish.

sunshine fruit risotto

THIS IS A REALLY COLORFUL RECIPE IN BOTH PRESENTATION AND FLAVOR. CHOOSE FRUITS AT THEIR PRIME.

5 cups (1.25 L) pineapple juice

¼ cup (50 mL) butter

2 Tbsp (25 mL) soft brown sugar

2 cups (500 mL) arborio rice

1 tsp (5 mL) ground cinnamon

1 tsp (5 mL) allspice

8 oz (225 g) fresh pineapple, peeled, cored, and cubed

2 bananas, peeled and sliced

1 papaya, halved, seeded, and sliced

1 mango, peeled and sliced

1 Pour the pineapple juice into a saucepan and bring to a boil. Reduce the heat to a gentle simmer.

2 Meanwhile, melt the butter in a large skillet and stir in the sugar and rice. Add the spices and cook gently, stirring, until the rice is well-coated in butter.

3 Add a ladleful of pineapple juice and cook gently, stirring, until absorbed. Continue adding pineapple juice in small quantities for 20 minutes. Stir in the fruit and cook for a further 5 minutes until the risotto is thick but not sticky. Serve in a warm dish.

apple, pear & cinnamon risotto

THIS IS A REAL ORCHARD DESSERT, DELICATELY FLAVORED
WITH CINNAMON TO BRING OUT THE BEST IN THE FRUITS.

5 cups (1.25 L) apple juice

1/2 cup (50 mL) butter

2 tsp (10 mL) ground
cinnamon

2 Tbsp (25 mL) soft brown
sugar

2 cups (500 mL) arborio
rice

2 red dessert apples,
cored and sliced

2 dessert pears, cored and
sliced

1/4 cup (50 mL) pecan
halves

1 Pour the apple juice into a saucepan and bring to a
boil. Reduce the heat to a gentle simmer.

2 Meanwhile, melt half of the butter in a large skillet
and add the cinnamon, sugar, and rice. Cook gently,
stirring, for 2 minutes until the rice is coated in butter.

3 Add a ladleful of apple juice and gently cook,
stirring, until absorbed. Continue adding apple
juice in small quantities until the risotto is thick but not
sticky, about 25 minutes.

4 Meanwhile, melt the remaining butter in a separate
skillet and cook the apples, pears, and pecans for
3 to 4 minutes, stirring. Add the fruit and pecans to the
rice, mix gently, and serve.

Index